Stephen Carleton Rogers
Box 145
Ossipee, New Ham

3.00

5720 Le Jeune Drive

D1254880

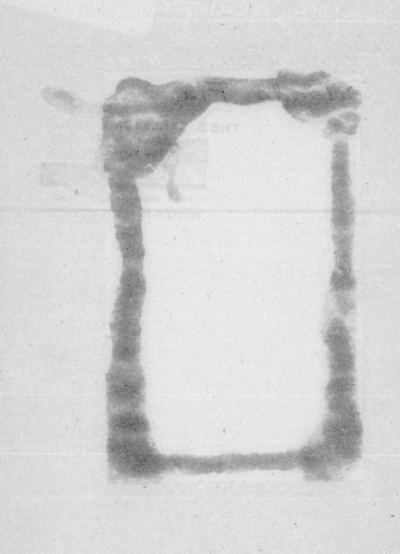

THE ART OF BIRD PHOTOGRAPHY

By the Same Authors

INTIMATE SKETCHES FROM BIRD LIFE
BIRDS OF THE DAY

The hen Montagu's-harrier flying low over her nest before alighting.

THE ART OF
BIRD PHOTOGRAPHY

WRITTEN AND ILLUSTRATED BY

ERIC J. HOSKING, F.R.P.S., M.B.O.U.
PHOTOGRAPHIC EDITOR, "THE NEW NATURALIST"

AND

CYRIL W. NEWBERRY, B.Sc., F.R.P.S.
PAST PRESIDENT, DERBY PHOTOGRAPHIC SOCIETY

LONDON: COUNTRY LIFE LTD.
2-10 TAVISTOCK STREET, W.C. 2

First published, 1944

BOOK
PRODUCTION
WAR ECONOMY
STANDARD

*This book is produced in
complete conformity with the
authorised economy standards*

PRINTED IN GREAT BRITAIN BY ROBERT MACLEHOSE AND CO. LTD.
THE UNIVERSITY PRESS, GLASGOW

Contents

71-71

List of Illustrations

Foreword

As an outcome of our recent book, *Intimate Sketches from Bird Life*, we have received a number of requests for a book on the art of bird photography, and the present volume is in answer to this demand. It is written to interest the ordinary man and woman, the schoolboy and the schoolgirl, who delight in seeing the wild birds around them and who would like to watch more closely, and sometimes photograph, the fascinating life of the feathered throng.

The book is practical in its outlook and caters for all types of bird photographers, including those whose spare time is limited and whose watching must be done in week-ends and evenings with perhaps a few consecutive days at holiday times. It deals with the art of seeing without being seen, and of photographing a naturally timid quarry without arousing its suspicions or causing it to behave unnaturally. Chapters are devoted to the equipment desirable for bird watching and for photography, and the various aspects of photography itself are dealt with in detail.

Some materials, as, for example, film packs, are temporarily unobtainable and some phases of nature photography, particularly flashlight work at night, are unfortunately out of the question for the duration of the war, but, for the sake of completeness, they are mentioned in this book. Flashlight photography has, in fact, figured largely in our correspondence, and we shall be gratified if our readers find in it the same fascination that we have found. It is a subject full of possibilities because of its ability to reveal what the eye cannot see. We recall, for example, the long-eared owls (plate 35), which are able to hunt and continue feeding their young throughout even the darkest night. The camera was able to secure a complete record of their food during several nights, though we ourselves were scarcely aware of their return to the nest, and could certainly discern no details of their actions.

While the majority of the book is devoted to bird photography, it is recognized that the bird lover will almost certainly be interested in the flowers, trees and insects that he sees in the course of

9

his wanderings, and which, on account of their interdependence, cannot be dissociated from bird life. Accordingly some space is devoted to the photography of the plant and animal life of the wayside and woodland, and it is hoped that the volume will be of interest and help to the many who, like our correspondents, love the wild life of the countryside and seek to record it with the camera.

E. J. H.

March 1941.   C. W. N.

War conditions have delayed the publication of this book, but recent changes in photographic emulsions have led us to vary our plates and films since the book was written, these changes have been incorporated in the text, which has thus been brought up to date.

Additions have been made to chapters XI and XIII to include our more recent experiences in the cinematography of birds and in the use of modern colour materials, and some of our latest photographs have been added.

E. J. H.

February 1944.   C. W. N.

I

In Quest of Birds

It is a common experience that as we roam the fields and byways, the abundance of wild life, that is known to be around us, seems to disappear at our approach. We see the rabbits nibbling at the turf in the distance and the birds flitting in and out of the bushes some fifty yards away, and yet, as we know only too well, unless special precautions are observed, we cannot approach them closely. Our progress is marked as it were, by an evacuation of the more mobile creatures from our immediate vicinity. The timidity of most birds and animals is an essential part of their make-up and we must recognize it as such; as a factor contributing to the survival of the species; and though to some of us it may be disappointing to be so shunned by the wild creatures, we, who wish to watch wild life at close quarters must accept it as a challenge to our art.

For many of us, the first experience of intimate bird watching comes in our own gardens. Sitting at ease in a deck chair in the quiet of a summer evening and glancing up from the pages of an absorbing novel, who has not had the thrill of seeing some little wild creature on the lawn at his very feet? It may have been the handsome chaffinch feeding on the turf, or the nimble little field mouse making his way along the border, but, whatever it was, we shall probably remember it vividly to this day. Through inexperience, however, our thrill will probably have been brief. Most of us will have yielded to the impulse to turn the head quickly to get a better view, or will have put down our book in a moment of distraction, and the timid visitor, mistaking our intentions, will have left hurriedly for shelter. Thus, we shall already have had our first lesson, that keeping still is in itself a valuable form of camouflage.

That is a beginning, but immobility is of course a serious hindrance to observation, and the naturalist must learn by experience how far he can allow himself some degree of freedom when near his quarry, without at the same time making it suspicious of his presence. He will find that he can, in fact, turn his head and move his limbs without frightening a nearby bird or animal, provided he moves only very slowly and avoids all jerkiness in his actions. The liberty that can be taken depends of course on the temperament of the particular bird that is being watched, and on his proximity to it, but a few examples will readily show what can be expected.

Sitting at lunch one day on a road-side bank, we were able to watch a pair of robins busily feeding their family less than fifteen feet away, and they took not the slightest notice so long as we remained seated. They were, however, hesitant to return when we stood up and moved about. Long-tailed tits on the other hand have ignored us completely when we have walked within a few feet of their nest. As a general guide it would be safe to say that most of the smaller birds can be watched in comfort at a distance of about thirty feet, provided the observer sits in some sheltered position such as against the trunk of a tree or under the shadow of a hedge. At that distance he can move head and arms with little restraint and without fear of upsetting the birds, and he is therefore able to use binoculars and make notes without hindrance.

With these elementary facts in mind, let us set out for an afternoon's observation in the field, for a little practical experience will soon teach us a good deal about bird watching. We take with us a notebook and pencil, and, if we have them, a pair of binoculars or field glasses. There is, in normal times, a wide range of glasses on the market and some are much more suitable than others for bird watching. In buying a pair, we insist first of all on a large field of view as this facilitates the observation of birds in flight. High magnification is less important, but we suggest a linear magnification of about seven or eight times with standard binoculars, or up to ten times with the special lightweight models. With greater magnifications it is difficult to hold the binoculars steady for any length of time.

Passing down a narrow country lane, we notice the hedgerows are alive with birds, but that most of the activity seems to be a little way ahead of us. Chattering yellowhammers scold us from the hedge tops, and tits and finches herald our approach. We are seeing one phase of bird life; the state of alarm at the approach of an intruder. In such conditions, little is to be seen of the fascination of the bird as an individual and we never come into intimate contact with his life.

Presently we come to a gate by the roadside, and pause to lean on it. A rough cart track leads across the field in front of us, and takes our gaze to the far side, where tall elms stand as sentinels above the hawthorn hedge. The ground is rough with tussocks of coarse grass, and here and there clumps of gorse break the view. Soon they take our attention as a pair of bullfinches disappear into their prickly depths. Here is a scene full of possibilities for the bird watcher, so, quietly pushing open the gate, we steal in a little way and sit under the shelter of the roadside hedge. At first there is little activity, but after a short while the slight disturbance of our entry to the field has been forgotten, and we see a bewildering kaleidoscope of little birds, moving hither and thither, it seems, without purpose. But as we watch, a certain repetition of movement becomes apparent. The bullfinches have dived again into the same gorse bush as when we stood by the gate; a little blue tit has several times made the journey between the gorse and a tree somewhere on our right, and a reed bunting has frequently been seen returning to a particular tussock of grass.

It is June, the middle of the nesting season, and these frequent journeyings are occasioned perhaps by the persistent clamourings of hungry families of chicks. Our present purpose is not specifically to locate nests, but rather to see as much as possible of the free movement of the birds around us; but we cannot help feeling the attraction of these handsome bullfinches, and our curiosity urges us to see their nest. If wise, however, we resist the temptation to walk across to the gorse, and restrain ourselves quietly in the shadow of the hedge. The activity in front of us continues, and, the longer we remain still, the more our presence in the vicinity is forgotten. More timid birds such as rook and magpie come down to feed not far away, and peewits return to this field where they lately nested.

Very little experience of this kind will impress on the beginner the importance of remaining inconspicuous if he would see the wild things as they really are, and he will, at the same time, have learned that keeping still is the greatest single factor in being inconspicuous from the birds' point of view.

Presently the time approaches when we must consider returning home; when we shall have, in any case, to disturb the peaceful activity in front of us; so turning our thoughts once more to the bullfinches, we decide to see their nest before we leave. Having watched them to and fro a number of times, we have a good idea of its situation, but from our viewpoint have not been able to fix it exactly; so, choosing a time when they are both away feeding, we move as unobtrusively as possible to another vantage point. This is selected with a view to seeing the birds' final approach to the nest, and, not until we are fairly sure of its location to within a yard or two, do we thrust ourselves into the open and make a search.

The way home takes us through a wood, so, in the hope of seeing as much as possible, we advance quietly in single file. Ears as well as eyes are on the alert for anything of interest, for we must learn to interpret the signs and sounds of the countryside as indications of bird activity. The experienced countryman misses nothing. The scolding of the wren may indicate the presence of a stoat, and a mobbing chorus of little birds may suggest an owl in the vicinity. Claw marks in the mud, and a few feathers strewn by the wayside, all tell their story, and, with increasing experience, the bird watcher will rely more and more on such indications to help him in his quest of birds.

II

How to Find Nests

It is for only a few weeks each year that the nest has any interest or meaning for the majority of birds, yet in that short period it is the focus of so much animation, there is little wonder that bird watchers and photographers have made it the centre of much of their observation.

It appears, from correspondence we have had, that many people have considerable difficulty in finding nests of even the common species of birds. To some the task seems as difficult as searching for a needle in a haystack, so in the next few pages we will try to indicate how the search may be made more fruitful. The example of the bullfinch that was used in the first chapter suggests one of the best methods of finding nests that are situated in bushes, trees and hedgerows. It is true that nests in such positions may sometimes be found by straightforward searching, but the technique of sitting quietly on one side, while the birds themselves reveal their own nests, is much more interesting, and will usually prove of more value in the long run. By this method several nests can generally be located at the same time, and, what is more, attention can be concentrated on just those species that it is desired to observe.

Straightforward searching is a method that can often be pursued in the course of incidental roaming about the countryside. It is most effective in the early part of the nesting season when the trees and hedges are still somewhat bare of foliage, and it must often be relied on to discover nests while they are being built. In this connection we should mention that clues, such as the carrying of nesting material, should of course be followed up if the observer is at all interested in the bird that is seen at the task. In searching a hedge, especially if it is still somewhat bare, it is usually an advantage to walk on the shady side and to look towards the light. In this way the dark mass of a nest will often be shewn prominently in silhouette, whereas it might pass unnoticed if seen against a dark

15

background. Later in the season, when the nest has been in use a little while, the increasing foliage may hinder direct inspection of the hedge, but a clue may sometimes be found in the litter of white droppings from the cock bird as he mounts guard on a favourite perch in the vicinity.

In the case of birds that nest on the ground, we have two peculiar difficulties with which to contend. The first is that the nest is usually well hidden in a tussock of grass or herbage, or else is so well camouflaged that we may often stand almost over it and yet fail to see it. The second difficulty is that many of these birds do not return direct to their nests after a flight. They alight on the ground some distance off and carefully pick their way through the undergrowth, often by a zig-zag route, so that it is impossible to follow them to the nest. To find these ground nests, the surest way is to tramp across likely haunts of these birds and to watch carefully ahead for a sitting bird to rise. If two or three friends are working together, and for many reasons bird watching is most effectively carried out by such co-operation, the manoeuvre is made much more effective by spreading out to about five yards apart and beating a relatively wide path across the territory. Nests of such birds as skylark and tree pipit, reed bunting and snipe, may often be discovered in this way, but an elaboration of the method is necessary in the case of the more timid ground nesters.

Almost as soon as anyone enters the marshes where peewit and redshank nest, the birds will be on the alert, and very soon will be wheeling overhead, shrieking their annoyance at the intrusion. It is therefore usually difficult to estimate the point from which any bird has risen, and the approach must be carefully planned to secure results. The first visit to the marsh will probably give the bird watcher a fair idea of where a nest may be found, and he may probably be tempted to try his luck at finding it; but even a ten yard circle can take a lot of searching if the vegetation is at all luxuriant, and often he will have to give up the hunt. The plan then is to retire for a while to let the wild life re-settle on the marsh, and then, after a suitable interval, to re-approach it stealthily, with a companion. Keeping under cover as much as possible and certainly keeping behind a dyke or ridge that will screen them from the

he robin we watched during lunch. Photographed from a standard hide, erected five feet from the nest,

Pl. 1.

Cyril Newberry watching from a sheltered position.

A skylark mounts guard on a favourite perch.

Pl. 2.

The dotterel is a rare bird which, in Great Britain, nests only in mountainous districts, more than 2,500 feet above sea-level.

Pl. 3.

A peewit's nest found by the method described on page 16.

The great spotted woodpecker's nest is often revealed by the litter of newly excavated wood round the bottom of the tree.

Pl. 4.

marsh itself, the two take up positions some distance apart. At a given signal, they emerge together into view of the nest. The sitting bird will probably leave almost at once, and each takes a careful bearing on the point from which she appears. Each may be a long way out in his estimate of distance, but if their eyesight is keen enough to spot her as soon as she rises, and if their courses are carefully noted, they will converge almost exactly at the nest, and its ultimate discovery should present little difficulty.

Finally, we have to consider those birds that nest in holes and crevices and such places that are difficult of access. Many of the nests must be found by following up clues suggested by the birds themselves. In one respect this is not so difficult as it sounds, for many of the birds that nest in holes are among the most striking of our British species. The outstanding example, of course, is the kingfisher, but the woodpeckers and tits come to mind as birds that are readily recognized in the field, while the barn and tawny owls can scarcely pass unnoticed. In looking for nesting holes in trees, the beginner will be struck by the large number of possible sites, many of them being disused nests of earlier years, but he can often make a rough inspection of a wood by noticing the entrances to likely looking holes. A tangle of cobwebs would at once suggest that a hole was not in use, but recent excavation, the presence of hair or feathers, or other unnatural material, would draw his attention to a nest, and further proof may be forthcoming if he taps the tree with a stick and then watches quietly for a while. A resident may look out to see who is causing the disturbance. A useful accessory in examining holes and crevices is a small piece of mirror mounted at the end of a stiff wire or piece of stick. With the aid of this and a flash lamp, it is possible to see into places that would otherwise be quite inaccessible.

These are a few suggestion for nest finding and will give the beginner something to start on. There is, however, nothing like experience in reading the signs of the countryside, and the intuition that comes of practice in seeking out birds.

B

III

The Hide and Other Equipment

In order to watch or photograph a bird at close range, we must use some device to screen us from the visual perception of our quarry. Such a device is usually called a 'hide'.

Hides may be of many different forms, according to the particular purposes for which they are used and the personal preferences of the bird watcher. A few people like to embark on bird watching with very little preparation and to improvise their hides in the field, but the majority prepare some form of hide which can be easily erected and which can be used repeatedly. In the past, elaborate forms of hide have been constructed to represent trees and cattle, but experience has shown that such representations of natural objects are quite unnecessary, and, as they are cumbersome and not readily adaptable, they are no longer used.

Before proceeding to a description of our own equipment, it will be of interest to review the desirable qualities of a hide and the features that make it acceptable to the bird. It must of course be sufficiently opaque to make the photographer quite invisible, even under those conditions when it comes between the bird under observation and the sun. It must be rigid to withstand adverse weather, and must be so constructed that no part of it can flap in the wind. We have previously seen that wild creatures will approach us if we keep still, but will not tolerate noticeable movement. They adopt the same attitude to a hide, and unless it is well constructed to resist movement, it may fail altogether as a means of approach to the bird, and will in any case prove to be a source of continual suspicion.

For convenience in working, the hide should be of sufficient size to accommodate the observer with some degree of comfort and yet should be readily transportable. It should be durable to stand repeated erection and dismantling, and yet be easily and quickly erected so that this operation will not cause unnecessary disturbance in the vicinity of a nest.

18

These demands may sound rather exacting, but they can in fact be satisfied fairly easily, and a form of hide that we use, and which was shown to us by our friend Ian M. Thomson, has proved so satisfactory for general work over many seasons that we cannot do better than explain its construction. It consists of four uprights, driven into the ground at the corners of a 3 foot square, and linked at their upper ends by stout wires as shown in fig. 1*a*, with a fitted cover of some suitable material. The four uprights are each 6 feet long and 1 inch diameter. The top of each is fitted with a brass ferrule to which are soldered two small tubes as shown in fig. 1*b*. These tubes are of suitable size (about $\frac{3}{16}$th inch inside diameter) to receive the ends of the wires joining the tops of the poles. A satisfactory size of wire is 10 gauge, and it should be galvanized to prevent rusting. It is a great convenience for packing and carriage

if the poles are jointed (fig. 1*c*), and if this is done, it is advisable to fit brass sleeves to both pieces of the pole to avoid an overtight joint when the wood becomes damp, as it surely must in service. The bottom of the poles should of course be pointed to facilitate driving them into the ground, and to make them last satisfactorily, we fit them with cricket stump spikes.

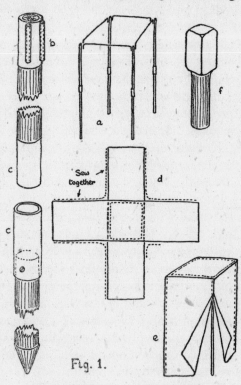

Fig. 1.

The cover of the hide is easily made from 10 yards of cheap casement cloth about 40 inches wide. A dull colour, either brown or green should be chosen, not so

Diagramatic construction of hide.

much to suit the fancy of the bird, as to make the hide inconspicuous when it is erected. A hide that advertises itself unduly may attract inquisitive strangers at a time when the photographer least wants them. The length of material should be cut in two, and the pieces laid on the floor in the form of a cross as shown in fig. 1*d*. The two are sewn together to form a double thickness in the middle. This double part forms the roof of the hide. The arms of the cross are then turned down and sewn together, as indicated, to form the sides. One seam should be sewn only for about 18 inches at the top so as to leave an entrance as shown in fig. 1*e*. Three or four strong safety pins will be needed to pin the door flaps together and to hold the cover tightly round the frame, and a few skewers are often useful to hold the bottom of the fabric firmly to the ground. A light mallet should be included in the equipment to facilitate driving the poles in hard or stony ground, for, if the poles are not well driven the finished hide will lack rigidity. A very useful accessory is a small hardwood peg like that shown in fig. 1*f*. This is dropped in the brass sleeve to prevent its being damaged when the bottom half of the pole is being driven. Finally, to provide against particularly rocky ground such as may be encountered on the bed of a mountain stream, we usually carry four guy ropes with us, and attach them if necessary to the tops of the poles. A hide constructed in this way will pack up into a bundle about 3 feet long by 6 inches across, and will weigh about 8 lb. It can, if necessary, be strapped to the crossbar of a bicycle.

The beginner may wish to start with one hide and get some experience with that before extending his equipment, but when he has settled down, and perhaps adapted the hide to suit his personal fancy, he will probably be inclined to construct several more. A worker with only limited time for bird study would manage quite well with two or three hides, while anybody devoting his whole time to bird watching would with advantage use about eight. The novice may wonder how he could ever use several hides at once, so looking ahead a little to what properly comes in a later chapter, we should make it clear that while only one hide is occupied at a time, the others are erected at other nests so that the birds may get accustomed to them.

In addition to the hide, there are certain other items of equip-

ment that the bird watcher will wish to have. First and most important is the notebook, and since note taking can be a laborious
business if not carefully planned, it is worth spending a few
moments to consider what is required. Every worker will have his
own preference in this matter, but we favour a loose leaf book. It is
indexed and arranged according to species, all the observations at
any one nest being kept together. A number of pages are ruled off
with paragraph headings as indicated on page 23, and one of these
pages is utilized to start the record, and provide a summary, of each
nest studied. The advanced worker may not wish to fill in descrip-
tions of nest and birds, unless he notes some unusual feature, as
these details are fully recorded in the *Handbook of British Birds* and
other publications, but the beginner is advised to make complete
notes, and will find the process an aid to accurate observation. The
book should be of reasonable size to obviate the too frequent
turning of pages, but it should certainly be small enough to slip into
a pocket so as to be always handy. We choose a stiff or semi-stiff
cover to facilitate writing in the hide. Another article, almost as
essential as the notebook, is a stool. This should be of the folding
variety unless transport is no problem, but it is a mistake to get one
of flimsy construction. It will sometimes be used on rocky, uneven
ground, and sometimes in a marsh, and only a strongly constructed
article will stand up to this treatment. It is important to make sure
that the stool is comfortable and of such height that the user can sit
without feeling cramped, for a lot may depend on the ability to sit
motionless for considerable periods. How vividly one of the
authors recalls one day sitting in a hide at a jay's nest. The young
jays were sleeping peacefully, when, without warning, there was a
clatter of wings among the branches just above the hide. One of the
parents had returned, but either she was in no hurry to attend to the
chicks, or else she was, for some reason or other, suspicious of the
hide. He knew her to be a wary bird and dare not move a muscle
for fear of increasing her suspicions. Ten minutes went by, and still
she sat above him; twenty minutes, and he badly wanted to ease the
cramp that was biting into one leg, but any move on his part would
have been magnified by the swaying of the hide on the slender
boughs that supported it, and must be avoided at all cost. The

ordeal spun out to thirty minutes, by which time a numbness and a
heaviness had come into the limb, and he could almost cry out
with the pain of it. Every minute seemed an hour as it dragged
slowly by, and still the jay sat, patiently waiting and watching.
Thirty-five, and even forty minutes passed, and the stool pressed
more and more deeply; into his very bones, it seemed; but he
matched his patience with that of the jay, and at last she came down
to the nest. He took the photographs, and fortunately got a good
series; but he learned more than bird photography that afternoon;
he learned to appreciate the importance of a good stool.

While dealing with equipment it will perhaps not be amiss to
include a few remarks on the question of clothing. It must be
adaptable to the wide range of occupations that go to make up
bird watching. That is, it must allow full freedom of movement for
strenuous walking and perhaps tree climbing, and should incident-
ally provide some protection against the thorns of bramble and
hawthorn, and the stings of nettle beds. A knitted woollen pullover
or jersey is excellent from many points of view, but the stitches are
readily caught and pulled in the course of tree climbing or wander-
ing amongst undergrowth, and it should usually be worn under a
leather jerkin or tweed jacket. Whatever is worn must, in particular,
be comfortable during long spells of sitting on the stool, and the
bird watcher must guard against anything that restricts the circula-
tion and accentuates the tendency to 'pins and needles'. An
adequate supply of pockets is very desirable, and one should be of
good size to accommodate the notebook. For protection against
rain we are never without an oilskin hat and a raincoat. The former
is particularly useful since it takes up no extra head room in the
hide and it folds away easily when not in use. Last, but not least
important, is the matter of footwear. Strong boots or shoes are
essential for general use, and a pair of plimsolls is an aid to tree
climbing, but, in addition, we strongly advise a pair of rubber
boots, as marsh land is a favourite nesting and feeding ground for
many species of birds. Lace-up boots, reaching to just below the
knee, are the most generally satisfactory, as they can be worn in
comfort for long periods and do not rub the heel to the same extent
as Wellingtons. Moreover, the fact that they are close-fitting

	Visits of		
	Cook	Hen	Food
Species: Song Thrush	30/4		
Location: Brown's farm, near Ipswich	7·23		not identified
Date found: 10/4/40		7·34	small earthworm
		7·46	snail?
Nest: Situation: In hawthorn hedge	7·50		slug
4 ft above ground		8·1	snail?
Material: Foundation of dry	8·57		flies
grass and leaves. Lining of	9·12		brown caterpillar
mud		9·19	snail
Eggs. Number: 10/4, 2; 11/4, 3; 13/4, 4		9·27	caterpillar
		9·35	"
Colour: Blue		9·46	earthworm
		10·4	flies
Hatching date(s) 26/4			
Cook: Length about 8 inches	10·16		snail
Colour of upper parts brown. Cheeks	10·29		—
buff, flecked with brown. Underparts		10·34	caterpillars
white, spotted dark brown on breast.	10·56		spider?
Bill dark brown, legs pale brown.		11·6	small snail
Hen: Similar to cock		11·17	centipede
	30/4		
		3·58	—
Periods of Observation: 30/4, 7–11·30 am.		4·27	brown moth
3·30 – 6·0 pm; 2/5, 10·0 am – 1·0 pm.		4·49	earthworm
4 – 7·15 pm; 7/5, 7·0 – 9·30 am.	5·7		
Remarks on Weather: Mainly fine		5·24	caterpillar
and mild			
General Remarks:		Continued overleaf	

Incubation Period: 13 days

Fledgling Period: not observed

Specimen page from field notebook.

reduces the risk of water overflowing or splashing into them when we have to work in shallow streams or dykes in search of moorhen, dipper, and birds that frequent such places.

As in most crafts, the personal equipment will reflect the needs and personality of the worker, and the many other non-essential items that could be included in the impedimenta of the bird watcher are best left to the whims of the individual.

IV

Photographic Equipment

Every photographer has his likes and dislikes in the matter of photographic apparatus, and, if a dozen of the leading Nature photographers were to be asked what cameras they prefer, it is probable that they would give nearly as many different answers. How then is the beginner to know what equipment he will require to do Natural History, and, in particular, bird photography? In the first place his choice is likely to be limited by questions of cost, and as the individual must ultimately be the judge of how much he is justified in spending on a camera, it would be useless for us to specify any particular apparatus as being necessary to the bird photographer. What we shall do is to explain the features that, in the course of a considerable experience of bird photography, we have found to be desirable, and to illustrate them by reference to our own apparatus. No one camera has even a passable performance over the whole wide range of bird photography, and accordingly, we use different cameras for different branches of the work; but after a consideration of their various points, we will indicate how a fairly wide range of photography can be achieved with a minimum of equipment.

By far the greatest part of our photography is close-up work from a hide, and for this we favour, without any hesitation, a field camera. Our own particular choice is an old ¼-plate Sanderson (plate 6), but any similar camera will serve the purpose. Screen focusing is almost essential for this branch of the subject, and the field camera combines this with several other important features. Among these may be mentioned provision for interchangeability of lenses, the lack of which rules out many small folding cameras; a rising and swing front, and a swing back; and a considerable bellows extension which, although not required in the hide, unless long focus lenses are to be used, renders the camera suitable for the making of close-up studies of small subjects in the field.

24

We are never without an oilskin hat and a raincoat. Note bottom of hide held down with stones. This hide was erected at the nest of a red-breasted merganser.

Pl. 5.

"LUC" SHUTTER

LENS

LENS HOOD

SWING BACK

Our field camera. Note lens hood with lip; 'Luc' shutter behind lens; long cable release; rising front and swing back; and tilting top on tripod.

Pl. 6.

*COURTSHIP
OF SLAVONIAN
GREBE.*

*An example of
photographs taken in
quick succession.*

*These three photo-
graphs were taken
in 12 seconds, this
being possible by
using film pack and
'Luc' shutter.*

Pl. 7

On leaving the nest the hen merlin accidentally kicked an egg out of the nest. It can be seen lying behind her. A fast panchromatic emulsion allows us to obtain a good depth of focus.

Pl. 8.

A lens of about 8-inch focal length is generally the most useful for working with this camera, or indeed with any ¼-plate camera for bird photography, and we have found the 8½ inch 'Serrac', made by J. H. Dallmeyer Ltd., excellent for the purpose. This lens has a maximum aperture of f4·5, which is plenty large enough for most work. For those occasions, and they are sure to arise, when it is impracticable to approach as close as we should like to our quarry, we carry a 12-inch 'Dallon' telephoto lens, made by the same firm, but, as far as possible, avoid using this long focus lens because of the small depth of focus and exaggerated perspective. Whatever lens is used, it should be fitted with an efficient lens hood. We use a tubular pattern which screws to the front of the lens and which has a projecting lip at its front end as may be seen in plate 6. As far as we know, such a hood is not marketed, but this was made specially for us so that, when the lens is pushed through the slit in the front of the hide, the lip prevents the hide fabric from slipping off and obscuring the camera lens.

The problem of a suitable shutter has worried many bird photographers, but as it happens, a shutter that is particularly easily adapted to the field camera is in fact the most suitable from several points of view. This is the 'Luc' shutter, illustrated in plate 6. It is of the three-bladed type, so arranged that pressure on the release causes the blades to open until they give the full aperture, after which continued pressure results in a rapid collapse of the blades to the closed position. This shutter is, for all practical purposes, silent until the final slight click at the moment of closing. Furthermore it needs no pre-setting, the length of exposure being controlled by the rapidity with which the release is pressed. The shortest exposure that can be given with this shutter is about $\frac{1}{30}$th of a second, but this is adequate for most birds at the nest, and the simplicity of control and silent working make this shutter pre-eminently suitable for bird photography. The release for this shutter is of the flexible cable type, about 20 inches long, which is very suitable for the bird photographer as it enables the shutter to be held at the ready for long periods without undue fatigue. As bought, these shutters are fitted with clamping screws for fixing them to the front of the lens, but we have found it preferable to have them adapted to screw on to the back of the lens mount, between the lens and the camera. This is a simple matter which can be readily undertaken by any instrument maker or camera repairer, and is worth the slight extra cost since it removes the moving blades from the immediate gaze of the bird, and at the same time protects the shutter from damage.

For the type of work that is being undertaken, a strong and rigid tripod is absolutely necessary, and it is important to see that it is continuously adjustable for height over as big a range as possible. The hide will probably have two apertures to accommodate the camera lens either high up or low down, but if the tripod is not readily adjustable to enable the lens to be fitted to one of these positions, it may be necessary to make fresh cuts for nearly every different nest, and the hide will rapidly become unserviceable. We use a fairly heavy wooden tripod as this stands up well to the conditions of service and is not readily damaged by having its feet pressed into sand or bog. In the confines of a hide, the disposition of the tripod feet is often somewhat limited, especially if the ground happens to be rocky and uneven. Under such conditions the tripod top often cannot be given just the desired tilt to suit the occasion, and a tilting top will be found to be indispensable. Ours is illustrated in the diagram (fig. 2), and can be copied by any handyman at the cost of a few pence.

The choice between film packs and plates is ultimately one for the individual user. There is no doubt that, when they can be obtained, film packs are better suited to the work because of the ease with which they can be manipulated, and the consequent speed and silence of working with them, and the fact that they are light and compact, but it must be admitted that they are expensive, and this feature may limit their use. Our advice to the beginner is to use film as much as possible because bird photography is an adventure; the unexpected is always happening; and the man who is unprepared for recording what may be a unique experience will always regret his missed opportunities. A point worth consideration is that the market for really good bird photographs is fairly extensive and the film pack will probably repay its extra cost by virtue of the occasional outstanding photographs that can be attributed to its

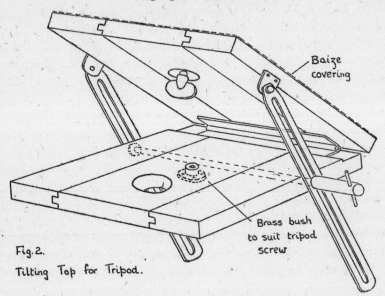

Baize covering

Brass bush to suit tripod screw

Fig. 2.

Tilting Top for Tripod.

rapidity of manipulation. The Slavonian Grebe, illustrated in plate 7, is a case where we took a series of photographs in quick succession. Another example is the change-over at the nest of the stone curlew, the story of which we recounted in *Intimate Sketches from Bird Life*. We took, at one part of the proceedings, a series of seven pictures in fifteen seconds. Such a feat could scarcely have been achieved, and certainly not in silence, had we been using plates. The same instance reminds us of one further point. We always carry two film pack adapters ready loaded so that, should it be necessary to start a fresh pack while a bird is on the nest, it can be done without having to rustle the paper and foil in which the film is usually packed. Moreover, if we anticipate a long series of exposures, we can remove a partly used pack and put it by for future use, while starting the series with a new pack giving us the possibility of twelve exposures in quick succession.

Whatever form of negative material is adopted, there can be little doubt about the emulsion required for bird work. It should always be of the panchromatic type, and it is usually best to choose a really fast material. Shady woodlands leave little margin for exposure on even the best of days, and in more open situations the fast emulsion is useful in permitting a control of the lens aperture to obtain a good depth of focus. We ourselves, generally use either the Selo Hypersensitive Pan or Kodak Super XX in filmpack form, and Kodak P1200 for the occasions when we resort to plates, as we are having to more and more during the war, and have found these to be very satisfactory for our purpose. The gradation and colour response of these emulsions are suitable for most bird work without the use of filters and, in general, we recommend the avoidance of these in the interests of exposure and depth of focus.

Among miscellaneous items of photographic equipment we do not hesitate to recommend the use of a photo-electric exposure meter. The nature of the subject, with its frequent wide range of contrasts and the widely varying conditions that are encountered, makes the estimation of exposure difficult for even an experienced photographer, and the beginner may well be puzzled by his complete inability to estimate the brightness outside a hide from his position inside. The difficulty arises largely from the fact that one eye, which has been looking out of the peep-hole in the hide, has its pupil contracted to suit the exterior light intensity, while the other eye, which has been looking at the inside of a comparatively dark hide, has its pupil somewhat dilated. The effect is demonstrated in no uncertain manner if, after a period of watching with one eye, the other eye is brought into use instead. The day will seem to change suddenly from dull into quite bright, or from bright into brilliant.

As an aid to critical focusing, which is specially important in technical subjects such as are being attempted, we suggest the use of a focusing magnifier, and, of course, we do not work without a focusing cloth. It is a good plan to have this specially large, say about 4 feet square, so that it can, in an emergency, be used as a background cloth or a wind break, as will be indicated in a later chapter.

While the field camera is so eminently suitable for work from the hide, it is, because of its bulk and the time taken in its erection, far from suitable for the miscellaneous shots that are encountered in the field, or for action pictures such as birds in flight. For such purposes we carry a miniature camera taking 35mm. film, choosing this size primarily because of the good range of film types available, including Kodachrome for the production of colour transparencies.

As in the case of the camera used from the hide, one feature that we consider of the greatest importance is the availability of a series of lenses of different focal lengths. In addition to the standard 5 cm. lens, we like a wide angle lens for views shewing typical habitats, and for photographing hides or other subjects in cramped situations where the camera cannot be placed far enough back to use the standard lens. We also use 9 cm. and 13·5 cm. long focus lenses, and find these especially useful for birds in flight. A large aperture is often necessary, as exposures must be brief to record the fine detail of wing feathers.

Good as the combination of field camera and miniature undoubtedly is, it does involve a considerable financial outlay, especially if each camera is fitted with a range of lenses. Many photographers will, accordingly, wish to confine themselves to one camera, and to these we cannot do better than recommend the equipment with which we began bird and nature photography, and which served us well for several years before the urge towards more specialized equipment reached a decisive stage.

Our trusty servant, and it still does useful work on occasions, was a ¼-plate Soho reflex. Owing to the limited head room in a hide, it could not be used as a reflex in such a situation, but focusing was carried out on the back screen in the same way as with the field camera. The 'Luc' shutter, which we now use on the latter, was used on the Soho and was fitted behind the 8½-inch lens. It should be noted that the more usual 6¼-inch lens which is fitted to ¼-plate cameras could not be used with the 'Luc' shutter behind it, as the lens would not then rack back close enough to the film. For general work where a silent shutter was not required, we used the 6¼-inch lens in conjunction with the focal plane shutter.

While this camera gave reasonably good results from the hide, it was also convenient for recording many of the miscellaneous subjects that we encountered unexpectedly in our wanderings. Slow flying birds could be shot (plate 40), but the camera was too heavy and unwieldy for other examples of bird flight, the indirect vision of the reflex being particularly awkward for rapid aiming of the camera at a fast moving bird; but as a good all-round camera for the bird photographer, the reflex has no equal. A point that should also be borne in mind by the beginner who chooses a reflex, is that when he feels the urge for more equipment, it is often possible to buy very cheaply a field camera without a lens. It is then a simple matter to have modifications made so that all the components, lenses, 'Luc' shutter, and plate-holders, will fit both cameras, and so have a flexible and versatile equipment at comparatively little cost.

V

Preparations for Bird Photography

Having discussed the equipment that is desirable for bird watching and for photography, we can now proceed to a consideration of the field work that will bring the photographer into intimate touch with his quarry. The beginner would be well advised to start work on one of the species which is quite plentiful, and to avoid the risk of disturbing any of the rarer birds until he has acquired skill and experience; but this will be no hardship. Many of the common birds provide thrills and tests of skill in plenty, and at the same time allow him to work within easy reach of his home. For many this latter point is of considerable importance, as good bird photography can seldom be achieved in a single outing. It is necessary to study the bird and to make preparations extending over several days to get the best results.

The first preliminary move to bird photography, after having made hides and assembled the necessary equipment, is to select a place to work. As mentioned above, it should be easily accessible so that it can be visited frequently, say sometime each day, or at least each week-end, but, especially in the vicinity of the larger towns, it is worth while taking a little trouble to obtain permission to work on private park or woodland, so that the quarry can be studied in as natural a state as possible, and without frequent disturbances. We have always found land owners to be extremely generous to us in the way of affording us facilities for study. There is little the photographer can do to repay their kindness; but we have often found that they welcome the gift of an album containing photographs of the wild life on their estates, and commend this as an appropriate way in which the photographer can show his appreciation.

We get to know the tenants and other workers, for with their knowledge of the locality they may be able to point out things that interest us. We listen to what they have to say, but do not neces-

31

sarily believe everything we hear. Imagination and hearsay enter
into many a yarn, and besides that, many a photographer has been
the victim of a good-humoured leg-pull at the hands of a keeper.
Good fellows these keepers are as a rule. They know their job and
work hard at it, and if their daily task brings them into touch with
few other folk, who can blame them for a bit of fun when the
opportunity occurs?

We accompany the keeper one day when he is on his round, and
make a mental note of likely haunts of various species; and it will
be strange if he doesn't point out to us an old hollow tree where an
owl has nested for many a year, or a plantation where, 'you'll be
sure to find a hawk'. But let beginners start on smaller fry, and,
remembering the lessons of the first two chapters, select the nests of
long-tailed tit and robin for the first attempts at bird photography.
Most bird photographs are taken at a nest, a favourite perch, or
some other known rendezvous where the bird may be expected to
alight at not too infrequent intervals. The nest is, without doubt,
the easiest situation, so for the present we will confine ourselves to
it. The long-tailed tits' nest is in a gorse bush, and, although five
feet high, it can be worked satisfactorily from one of the standard
hides. The robin is low down, hidden in the vegetation of a low
bank surrounding a spinney, so that she, too, can be photographed
from another standard hide. We mark the positions of each of these
nests by a small pile of stones, or a stick pushed into the ground, or
whatever method seems suitable for the particular situation,
making the sign sufficiently definite so that we shall recognize the
spot again, and yet not so conspicuous that it will attract attention.

Both nests contain young chicks, so, at the first opportunity, we
return to our hunting ground laden with two hides (and a spare one
if we can carry it), the mallet and peg, and a few safety pins, and, of
course, binoculars and notebook. We come first to the nest of the
robin and quickly set to work to erect one of the hides, not in the
working position, but about twelve feet in front of the nest. The
poles are driven firmly into the ground, the connecting wires
dropped into the sockets, and the cover put in place. The door flaps
are pulled tightly together and fastened with a few safety pins, and
skewers are pushed into the bottom of the hide to keep it from

airig Ghru Pass; a typical example of the use of wide angle lens on the miniature camera.

NEST

Hide and habitat of capercaillie (see plate 48). An example where wide angle lens was essential.

Pl. 9,

Greenshank hide. Preliminary erection at half-height.

Greenshank approaching chicks.

Pl. 10.

Greenshank removing eggshell from nest.

Greenshank at nest. Note shell remains and chicks. Examples of three different nests of the same species. Repeat observations are necessary in our study of bird life.

Pl. 11.

THE ERECTION OF THE LONG-TAILED TIT HIDE.

The first stage. A case where the environment precluded the more usual procedure of first erecting the hide some distance from the nest.

The long-tailed tit hide. Stage two.

NEST

The long-tailed tit hide, ready for use.

Pl. 12.

The long-tailed tit's nest after completion of the 'gardening'.

Pl. 13.

Peewit settling on eggs. When properly focused the nest usually occupies about one quarter the width of the picture.

Pl. 14.

Whinchat on perch arranged near nest.

Pl. 15.

A hide and ground nest surrounded by a fence to protect them from cattle.

Eric Hosking with rolled-up hide and photographic equipment.

Pl. 16.

blowing about. As soon as we are satisfied that the structure is secure against any wind that may get up, we leave the vicinity to allow the robins to return to their nest and to accustom themselves to the new erection.

Taking the other hide with us, we go across to the gorse where the long-tailed tits were found. Our mark helps us to locate the nest. We examine it, noting the position of the entrance and the presence of any likely stems of gorse that the birds may use as perches as they approach. These give an indication of the best viewpoint from which to take our pictures, but the direction of the light at the time of day when we shall be able to watch these birds must also be considered. This may force us to modify the viewpoint to some extent to avoid photographing directly against the light. During these preparations, the tits are flying close by, mobbing us a little, maybe, because we are closer to the nest than they like, but showing how readily they would return if only we would go a little farther away; so a start is quickly made on the erection of the hide. As in the case of the robin, it should first be erected a little way from the nest, to let the birds get used to it at a distance, but we find that other clumps of gorse prevent us from getting back. Accordingly, the hide is built in stages, so that there shall not be too sudden a change in the environment.

The lower halves of the two front poles are driven so that they stand about five feet in front of the nest, in the direction from which we intend to take our pictures. The bottom halves of the other two poles are driven to complete the square, and the connecting wires are dropped into the jointing sleeves at the top of these pieces of the poles (plate 12). This is enough disturbance to begin with, and the top halves of the poles, together with the cover of the hide, are concealed under a nearby bush until next day, while the tits accustom themselves to the bare framework.

This completes our first day's preparations at these two nests, so we leave the vicinity of the hides and spend the rest of our time in general observation of the things around us, and in recording in our notebooks what has been done. It may well be that, in the course of our further wanderings, we discover some other nest to photograph and this is where the spare hide comes in useful. Let us suppose that

c

it is a peewit's nest with eggs, for this will give us a real test of our skill. The peewit, although common in most districts, is usually very shy, and we must, therefore, take special care in approaching her.

The hide is first erected some thirty yards from the nest, but in view of the shyness of the bird, the openness of the situation and the lack of protection from wind, it is, in the first instance, only erected at half height. The frame is arranged in the same way as that at the tit's nest, but in this case, as it is some way from the nest, the cover is put on, the loose material at the bottom being rolled, and weighted down with stones or clods of earth. We finish the task as quickly as possible, and leave the hide looking very much like that shown in plate 10, which shows one that we used at the nest of a greenshank.

The next day, or as soon after that as can be managed, we re-visit the hides and advance them a stage towards completion. The robin hide is moved up to about five feet from the nest; the covering is put on to the half-poles by the tits, and is securely fastened down (plate 12); and the peewit hide is re-erected about fifteen yards from that nest, but still only at half height. This stage by stage technique in putting up hides is very important, and our observations and photographs will depend very largely on the care with which the preliminary work has been done. We do not recommend putting a hide directly in position at any nest, however bold the bird may appear to be. To do so would incur a grave risk of making the bird desert her eggs or chicks; and even if the effect were not so serious as that, it is probable that she would never overcome her suspicion of the hide, and her behaviour, in consequence, would not be completely natural. In the case of the smaller birds, and particularly those that nest in undergrowth and bushes where there is a fair amount of natural screening, it should be possible to complete the placing of the hide in three moves, or in very favourable circumstances, in two; but for a more timid species such as the peewit, to which we have referred, four or five moves are desirable to avoid making her unduly nervous. In the case of the larger predatory birds, the work should be done in four or five stages, or even more, and spread over a period of ten days or a fortnight, while there are instances, of which the heron is one, where the work cannot be done satisfactorily once the bird has occupied the nest, and the hide should be completed during the winter before the herons have returned to the heronry. From this it will be apparent why it is necessary that bird photography should be carried out within easy reach of the photographer's own home, or that he should stay for some time in the place where he intends to carry on his bird studies. Casual snapshotting can seldom produce results of any value.

To return, however, to the preparations we have in hand; on the third day the peewit hide can be moved another stage closer to the nest. It may now be, perhaps, within twenty feet, but much will depend on the temperament of the particular bird, and, until some experience has been gained, it is best to err on the safe side even if it delays the preparations a little. The robin hide is already in the working position, and we leave it for the moment and pass on to the long-tailed tits, which we are anxious to watch at the first opportunity. The hide may now be erected at its full height, but even when this is done it is advisable to defer photography for another day to let the tits settle quite happily.

A little preliminary 'gardening' may, however, be done where necessary. 'Gardening', in the language of the bird photographer, means the re-arrangement or removal of some of the foliage surrounding a nest in order to obtain a reasonable view of the nest from the hide, and possibly also to improve the lighting. In carrying out this operation, the photographer should always consider the bird. He should make only gradual changes in the nest environment and should avoid removing anything which is necessary to protect the nest from the sun or rain or from the attention of the birds' natural enemies. He will, of course, for his own sake, try to preserve the natural appearance of the nest as far as is compatible with obtaining a photograph.

At last the day arrives when we hope to begin our intimate study of the tits. As we make our way to the nest, they are flying to and fro, and even perching on the hide itself as well as on the gorse. Surely then, these little birds are in no way disturbed by our intrusion, and observation and photography can safely be started without fear of recording unnatural proceedings. We unpin the doorway and enter at the back of the hide to view the nest through the hole the camera lens will presently occupy. There is the nest nicely placed in front of us, but, in spite of the preliminary 'gardening', it is intentionally still partly obscured by a large stem of gorse some fifteen inches in front of it. This stem does nothing to support the nest, and would definitely spoil the photographs by being out of focus and of exaggerated size, so we might be tempted to cut it away. This, however, would be bad practice and should be avoided as much as possible. The stem serves a useful purpose in screening and shading the nest, so, in order that it can be replaced when we have finished photography, we pull it down gently and tie it out of the field of view of the camera. Looking again, we see that one or two small twigs are still rather obtrusive and would cast awkward shadows across the birds, but these can, without any detriment to the birds, be permanently removed. They are cut off cleanly in such a way that the general appearance of the nest surroundings are altered as little as possible, and so that the cut itself will not be obvious in the photograph. Points to bear in mind in this connection are to incline the cut so that the actual cut surface which tends to show up as a highlight, faces away from the camera, and, if possible, to position the cut so that it is hidden behind another stem or a leaf.

The 'gardening' around the nest completed, we turn our attention to preparations inside the hide; the erection and focusing of the camera and the settling of ourselves and equipment, but the photographic part of the job belongs to the next chapter, and before proceeding to that, it will be as well to consider a few other points that may confront us as 'preparations'.

One poser that confronts the beginner is, 'What is the most suitable time for erecting a hide?' The answer depends to some extent on the bird that is to be watched, and on the particular purpose of the watching. For example, it would be no use deferring the erection of the hide until the chicks had hatched if we were interested in the share taken by cock and hen in brooding; but putting other considerations on one side, the period just about the hatch is the time when the birds are most intent on their duties at the nest, and are, in consequence, least likely to be put off by a bird watcher's activities. During the building of the nest, and for the early part of brooding, the hen is more easily deterred from her purpose, and so, if preparations must be made at such a time, they must be undertaken with special caution.

Another question that is often asked is, 'How close to a nest should the hide be placed?' There is no one answer to this question, but a few general remarks will soon indicate how the answer may be found for any particular case. In the first place we must consider what is to be included in the photograph. It is a mistake to get so close that the bird fills the picture. This is usually neither pleasing pictorially, nor satisfying from a technical point of view, as the nature of the surroundings are of definite interest. Until experience has been gained in the art of bird photography, the best way of siting a hide is to test with the camera that will be used. This helps, not only in arranging the hide at the right distance, but in so placing it that the nest is seen, if possible, against a suitable background. The bird photographer usually has little choice in this matter, but he should always try to avoid 'spotty' or dazzling backgrounds of high contrast, such as result from sky showing through a tangle of twigs and leaves. When properly focused, the nest usually occupies about one quarter of the width of the picture. If, however, the lens is of comparatively short focal length, the photographer may have to be content with a rather smaller image on the negative, as it is rarely advisable, even with small, confiding birds, to work closer than about four feet. In the case of birds like the peewit that was considered earlier, we usually bring the hide up to the nest, until it is within about seven or eight feet. Except in the case of nocturnal birds, this gradual approach is the more effective if the moves are made towards evening, when the fading light helps to conceal the new erection.

Hides, unfortunately, tend to arouse the curiosity of man and beast. As we remarked earlier, the hide should be drab coloured to make it inconspicuous to the former, but, if cattle or horses are at large in the field where it is erected, some further protection is usually necessary to preserve it from their attentions, and to prevent them from using it as a rubbing post. In such circumstances, we usually drive four strong stakes into the ground and join them at a height of about three feet by barbed wire, which can usually be borrowed from a keeper or farmer. This simple fence should enclose both hide and nest if the latter is on the ground, as otherwise the attraction of the hide may lead to the destruction of the eggs. We need hardly remark that the fence should, of course, be arranged to be out of the camera field (plate 16).

Another preparation that might be mentioned is the provision, in some instances, of a suitable perch near the nest. This properly comes into a later chapter, but it is so closely related to photography at the nest that it can with advantage be referred to here. Many birds do not fly from a distance direct to the nest, but prefer to alight first in its immediate vicinity. This gives us an opportunity for what almost amounts to posing the bird, and often enables us to arrange our 'sitter' against a less distracting and simpler background pattern than the nest usually affords. In such a case it is desirable to remove any natural alternative perches in order to limit the bird to the use of the one point on which the camera is focused, but it must be remembered that this will, to a small extent, modify the bird's natural movements, and must be avoided if it would influence any feature under observation. It is purely a photographic artifice to achieve pleasing pictorial results, as shown in plate 15.

Finally, no account of preparations for bird watching or photography would be complete without a reference to the vast amount of study that has already been expended on these subjects. There is, without doubt, an enormous thrill to be got from the mere close-up watching of birds, but there is much more interest attached to the pastime if we watch with a purpose. Good books dealing with this branch of the subject are, *The Art of Bird Watching* by E. M. Nicholson, and *Watching Birds* by James Fisher, and we recommend the reading of these to all bird watchers. It is also as well to know something of what has been recorded previously about any species we intend to study. It is very difficult to take in all that is happening before our eyes, and to appreciate the significance of every little action, but if we have, to some extent, acquainted ourselves with the observations of others on the same subject, we can pick on some particular feature which seems worth further study and concentrate our attention on it. There are many books devoted to detailed studies of a few selected species, and well-informed articles appear regularly in the monthly journal *British Birds*, and the weekly papers *The Field* and *Country Life*, and we commend these to all who take a real interest in bird life; while in addition there is no better reference book than the concise and comprehensive *Handbook of British Birds*, which should undoubtedly be on the bookshelf of every bird watcher.

VI

Bird Photography from the Hide

(1) At the Nest

The first spell of watching from a hide is a never-to-be-forgotten experience. The expectant waiting till the bird returns, and then the thrill of seeing, at such close range, the detailed beauty of a creature from the wild, brings an excitement that almost numbs the senses. We hold our breath, not so much for fear of revealing our own presence, but because we are so absorbed in the spectacle before us.

The fascination of bird watching endures, even for the experienced observer, and in the face of this absorption in the events in front of him, the bird photographer is well advised to prepare his procedure down to the last detail. We try to reduce the demands of photography to the bare minimum so that we can devote as much attention as possible to observation and note-taking, and in what follows we record in some detail our own photographic procedure.

When all is prepared for photography, as indicated in the previous chapter, the photographer, with one or more assistants, proceeds to the hide and sets up the camera and tripod. The height of the camera is adjusted so that the lens can be pushed through one of the slits made in the front of the hide for the purpose, and the camera is roughly focussed on to the nest or perch where the bird is expected to settle.

As mentioned previously, we usually make two slits to accommodate the camera lens. One is about half way up the hide and is used for working nests that are on or near the ground and the other is near the top and is generally used for nests about three to five feet high. The arrangement of a slit rather than a hole for the camera lens has three important points in its favour; first, the lens is pushed through the slit until it projects an inch or so and this obviates any risk of the lens becoming obscured by the hide; secondly, the sides of the slit fit snugly to the lens mount and conceal the movements of the photographer when adjustments are made to the camera; and thirdly, the slit is readily closed by a safety pin when not in use.

The curlew brooding. The first time the bird returns to the nest, it is advisable to refrain from exposing. Let her brood for some while, then note her reactions to the sound of the shutter.

The curlew approaching nest. When the bird has accustomed herself to the sound of the shutter, exposures may be made during her subsequent approaches.

Pl. 17.

The fascination of bird watching endures. We meet the golden eagle.

Black-headed gull alighting at nest. An example of choosing the moment for exposure Field camera, shortest exposure with 'Luc' shutter. 8½" lens at f 8.

Pl. 18.

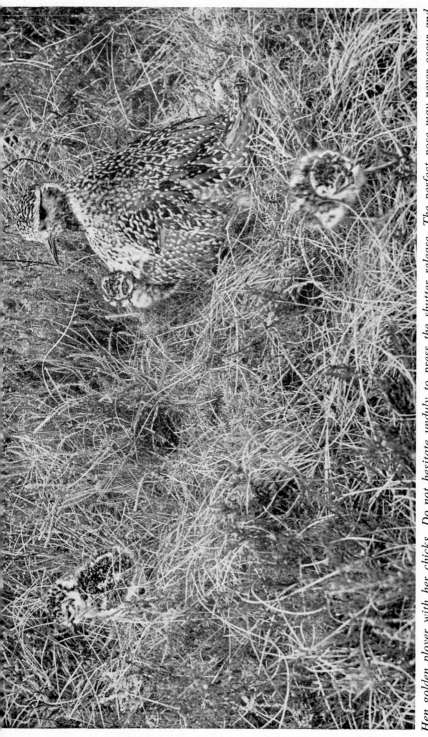

Hen golden plover with her chicks. Do not hesitate unduly to press the shutter release. The perfect pose may never occur and the photographer must seize opportunities as they occur.

Pl. 19.

A slight shift of the camera enabled us to photograph the crested tit perched just above its nest.

Pl. 20.

Having installed the camera, and got it focused, the photographer inspects the image on the focusing screen to see if any distracting high lights are produced by reflections from wet or glossy leaves, and checks that no avoidable out-of-focus foreground objects remain in the picture. These are either moved slightly until they no longer offend, or are carefully removed. When all outside preparations are complete the light intensity is measured with the exposure meter, and a mental note is made of the likely variations due to the passage of cloud. The lens aperture is adjusted, usually to about f11 or f16, if light conditions allow, and if the bird is not expected to be unduly rapid or jerky in her movements. The photographer then retires inside the hide to complete his preparations there.

We usually arrange the stool in the left hand front corner of the hide and have the camera, in consequence, disposed slightly to the right, but this is a matter of personal preference and sometimes has to be altered to get the best viewpoint for the camera. The camera case, with its stock of loaded plate-holders and film pack adapters is placed on the ground towards the back, but within easy reach; and close enough to be used as a temporary parking place for notebook, pencil and any odds and ends. If the ground is at all damp, it is advisable to cover the floor of the hide with a layer of bracken to protect the camera cases, and the stool is best stood on a piece of board, if this can be obtained. A mattress of sticks sounds attractive for this purpose, but should be avoided, as the sticks are liable to crackle, and usually do so at a critical moment.

While the photographer settles himself on his stool and cuts a small peep-hole in the front of the hide, (this, too, is usually a short slit and is held open by a piece of twig or a match-stick), an assistant pins up the doorway at the back. He waits by the nest until the photographer is quite ready; lens aperture adjusted to suit the light conditons; plate or film inserted and dark slide drawn; notebook on knee, and flexible shutter release ready to hand; and then, having arranged what time he will return to effect the release of his companion, he leaves the vicinity, making, as he does so, sufficient noise and commotion to emphasize his departure to deceive the wild life around into assuming that the hide has been deserted. Experience has shown that, with few exceptions, birds fail to distinguish between the two persons approaching a hide and the one leaving it. They seem to register danger approaching and then danger departing, and are satisfied.

The interval of time that elapses before the photographer becomes aware that the bird is returning varies enormously with different species, and even between birds of a species, so it is essential to keep a sharp look-out through the peep-hole. Small subsidiary peep-holes in the back and sides of the hide are of considerable help at this stage of the vigil, but they must be very small or they may have a marked influence in reducing the opacity of the hide, and so reducing its effectiveness. In spite, however, of the need for almost constant watchfulness, a start must be made in the note book, and this is where tabulated pages as illustrated in chapter 3, are of value in saving time and in ensuring a complete record.

At last the bird is approaching, and the beginner will anxiously finger his shutter release. The more experienced worker, on the other hand, will put aside the temptation to begin photography at once, and will allow a little time for the bird to settle herself and overcome any nervousness or suspicion she may have had concerning the camera and the hide, now that it is actually occupied. Her actions should be watched with interest and carefully recorded, but it must not be assumed that, at this first approach to the camera, her behaviour is entirely normal. Soon she will have settled comfortably, and the first exposure may be made, but, even then, the slight click of the shutter may cause her to start. She will probably lift her head and peer about for a while, and during this display of nervousness the photographer should avoid all movement, and postpone the adjustment of the film pack or the changing of plates until the bird has regained her composure. It will be found that, provided the photographer exercises his patience in the early stages of working on a particular bird, the bird will accustom herself to the slight incidental noises that are inevitable in the operation of the camera. When she has done so, considerably more liberties may be taken, and exposures may be made during her subsequent approaches and departures, and, in fact, a complete photographic record may be made of her in various attitudes and performing the various actions that comprise her life at the nest.

In any attempt to make a comprehensive record, the photographer must remember that the camera has been previously focused on some particular point, usually about the middle of the nest, and although, if he has stopped down to f11 there should be a fair depth of focus, he must avoid the temptation to expose when the bird is much beyond the focal distance, as for example, when she is approaching the nest. If, during a period of observation, he notices that there is the possibility of good photographs at some other point than that on which the camera is focused, it may be possible to re-focus during a period when the bird is away from the nest, but it is seldom advisable to move the camera unless only a very slight shift is required. Swinging the camera without moving the tripod can be done to only a limited extent because the lens position is more or less fixed by the slit in the hide, and moving the tripod is unwise because of the inevitable disturbance in the way of noise, and movement of the hide covering. The camera should not be re-set until the beginning of the next spell in the hide, or until any period when the photographer's colleague may have approached and created the necessary disturbance from outside.

In making exposures, the bird photographer should study the bird in front of him as closely as a portrait photographer studies his model, but he must not hesitate unduly to press the shutter release, because events which are worth recording may not be performed again in his presence. Often there is a tendency to put off the moment of exposure in the hope that the bird may move to a more favourable position or attitude, but, once the bird has become accustomed to the click of the shutter, our advice is to expose as soon as events justify it, and then to prepare quickly but quietly to expose again, if necessary. This is especially important if, for example, it is desired to record the food brought to the nest, or to picture some unusual happening.

Presently the allotted span of the vigil comes to a close and the photographer's companion returns to the hide. It may sometimes happen that a particularly interesting photograph is in prospect at such a time. For instance, the photographer may have secured a series of photographs of one bird only, and yet have observed that the other one of the pair is approaching the nest. It would be a great pity to disturb such a situation, so we always arrange a signal to indicate whether our relief should approach or not. If ready to be relieved, we tuck the corner of a white handkerchief through an opening in the back of the hide. If, at the appointed time, the handkerchief is not in position, the relief knows to delay his approach, and watches from a distance, usually through binoculars, for the signal to be displayed. It is most important that the photographer should not emerge by himself from what, from the point of view of the wild life around it, is an unoccupied hide, or he will arouse distrust and suspicion that will seriously influence his future prospects.

It will by now be appreciated how desirable it is for bird photographers to work in pairs, as although, in general, only one will be engaged in actual bird photography at a time, he cannot work without assistance. There is, however, plenty to keep two friends fully occupied, for while one is in the hide, the other can be finding nests for future working, or can, through binoculars, maintain a watch and record the activity at other nests where more complete observations are required on such matters as feeding habits and extent of territory. The photography of birds in flight is another possibility, and, in addition to this, there is a vast field of work on allied subjects, such as the study and photography of insects, flowers and trees, concerning which, more will be explained in a later chapter.

Up to this point our account has been devoted almost entirely to procedure, but there remain a number of more technical matters which should receive our attention. First and foremost, perhaps, is the vexed problem of shutter speed and lens aperture. For any particular value of the light, it is possible to obtain correct exposure of the negative from a wide range of shutter speeds, provided the lens aperture is suitably adjusted; but these do not all give the same result in the finished picture. We favour the longest exposure that can be given with safety; that is, without too much risk of the birds' moving during the exposure interval. This of course varies greatly with the nature of the bird, but, except in the case of small birds such as the tits, and some with special characteristics like the wagtail, it is often possible to give exposures of the order of one half to one tenth of a second. Such exposures permit the use of comparatively small lens apertures with the result that considerable depth of focus is obtained. In order to facilitate the attainment of sharp pictures with slow shutter speeds, we often try to 'freeze' the bird in the required attitude. This is done by making a slight scratching noise at the appropriate instant (just sufficient to take the bird's attention) and almost simultaneously pressing the shutter release.

While on the question of exposure, we might just refer to the lighting conditions that give the best results in bird photography. We try as far as possible to avoid direct sunlight. Our subject is almost always one of high contrasts, and a diffused, or even a dull light, is to be preferred, so long as it is sufficiently directional to give a suggestion of modelling. This condition usually obtains when the sun is obscured by light clouds. The question of contrast must be kept always in mind, and, especially if the light is at all strong, exposures should be on the generous side with a view to subsequent control during development.

During any one spell of watching from the hide we have recommended that the camera should remain focused on one particular spot. If we want, however, to obtain records of a bird at the nest and on a special perch as mentioned in the previous chapter, we either devote separate spells to the two positions, or use two cameras at once. The former alternative may often be very tantalizing, for, if the camera is focused on one of two places, the most interesting events always seem to take place at the other. One of our greatest disappointments was to miss the feeding of the little owl chick to which we referred in *Intimate Sketches*, but this is by no means an isolated example. There is, as a rule, not sufficient space in a hide to accommodate two tripods, so, when we want to use two cameras, we use a double tilting top, shown in plate 21, and fit the Sanderson with the 12-inch lens to one part, and the reflex with the 8½-inch lens to the other. The operation of the two cameras makes a fascinating pastime, but it demands considerable concentration and we do not recommend the practice to beginners.

VII

Bird Photography from the Hide

(2) *Away from the Nest*

The intense bird activity in the nesting season, coupled with the localizing influence of the nest itself, makes bird photography at the nest, as we have already suggested, a comparatively easy matter. The season is, however, rather short for most birds, and for the greater part of the year, we must, if we wish to continue our studies, go in search of a quarry that has no need to return to any precise spot. Accordingly, our approach must be the more skilful, and our technique modified to suit the altered circumstances.

Two possibilities are open to us. We may either entice the bird to appear in front of the camera, and then deal with it in much the same way as when it returned to the nest; or we may take the camera, preferably fitted with a telephoto lens, to a place known to be frequented by the birds it is hoped to photograph. The former is the easier, and more certain, method; but the latter, while less sure of producing results, is the more interesting, since it enables us to see another phase of bird life under natural and uncontrolled conditions.

Let us deal first with the problems involved in enticing the bird to the camera. The obvious thing that comes to mind is to use a feeding table, and, as many bird lovers will already have some experience of a bird table in the garden, it may be a good plan to consider this first as a focal point for our activities. For convenience in photography, the table should be rather low, say about three feet above the ground, so that the camera can point down slightly to it, and any rim which may be provided to prevent food from rolling off, should be quite shallow, or it may hide the bird's feet. The table itself should be quite small for several reasons. First, to confine the bird as closely as possible to one particular distance from the camera. Much of the photography at the feeding table will be done during the winter months, when, although the weather may be fine and sunny, the actinic value of the light is

46

comparatively small, and it will be necessary to use a large stop and have, in consequence, very little depth of focus. Secondly, a small table helps to locate the bird in the desired part of the picture space; and thirdly, it reduces the possibility of a large number of birds alighting at one time, and confusing the picture. The beginner might feel attracted by the possibility of photographing a large number of birds at once, but let him watch carefully a horde of greedy starlings, squawking and fighting over the scraps on the table, and he will soon realize the extreme difficulty of picking any instant when there is a reasonable lack of movement to allow the necessary $\frac{1}{5}$th or $\frac{1}{10}$th of a second exposure to be made.

The table should be set up and supplied regularly with food for some time before it is intended to begin work, so that the birds may become thoroughly accustomed to it. It is possible to take photographs from the warmth and comfort of the house if the table is placed about four feet from a window, but in such a situation the variety of species which will use it is comparatively small. Unless the window itself is made of good quality glass, it should be open when photography is attempted, but this will not cause undue distress throughout the house, as the window space should be 'blacked out', and there will be few extra draughts as a result of the photography. Material such as was used for the hides will be quite suitable, and it should be stretched tightly across the window frame and provided with a slit for the camera lens, and a small peep-hole.

Besides limiting the choice of species, bird photography from a window gives very little choice of background, unless an artificial one can be fitted up, and, in many instances, a serious lack of front lighting, so that it is usually preferable to place the feeding table well away from the house and to take the photographs from a hide. This should be arranged, if possible, rather to the south of the table so that the photographer gets the full benefit of the winter sunshine, but the actual position must be selected to give a suitable non-distracting background, and so that the hide itself does not cast a shadow on the table at the time of day when he will most frequently be able to work. Especially as he will be working a good deal in cold weather, we recommend, where practicable, that the hide should be rather more substantial than those described for general purposes. It need not be portable and can be built of wood and fitted with a small ledge table and possibly a heating stove. In fact, the more permanent it is, the better, both from the photographer's and the birds' point of view. We have found that a small tool shed serves admirably for this purpose. A peep-hole and a hole for the camera lens should be cut in the front, and, if there is a small window, this should be retained as an additional look-out, and to illuminate the interior, but it should be covered with a net curtain. If no stove is fitted, a very convenient alternative way of keeping warm is to sit in a sleeping bag pulled up to the waist and to have a couple of hot water bottles in the bottom.

In placing food on the table, the photographer should endeavour to provide as much variety as possible in order to attract different species of birds, but he must avoid the pitfalls of being too liberal at one time, or using unsuitable material, as either of these will distract attention from the bird itself. Nothing looks worse in a photograph than a large number of white blobs resulting from a liberal sprinkling of food scraps. It may be desirable to be more generous when the table or hide is first erected, in order to encourage birds, but once they have got into the habit of visiting the table, a small supply of finely crumbled pieces will bring them to the camera, and, in fact, the more finely divided the food is, the longer they will be tempted to stay in order to satisfy their appetites.

We need hardly mention the other variations on the feeding table idea—the pieces of coconut shell filled with fat and suspended for the tits, or the string of pea-nuts; but it is perhaps worth referring to the possibility of attracting some of the large predatory birds to a bait laid on the ground. We ourselves have had little experience of this particular work, but the method has been developed very successfully by H. G. Wagstaff. He erected a hide in a place well away from the possibility of human disturbance, and arranged with the local keeper to put out bait regularly over a long period. The bait usually consisted of a dead rabbit, which was pegged down firmly so that it should not be carried away whole by such birds as buzzard and raven. In due course, and by the exercise of considerable patience, he obtained very fine photographs of

A double tilting top is used to support two cameras.

Pl. 21.

Greenshank perched. Photographed with reflex camera and 12" telephoto lens. Tw[cameras used at once as indicated in Plate 21.

Pl. 22.

The greenshank at the nest.

Pl. 23.

The cock Montagu's harrier visits the hen at the nest. This and the companion pictur *illustrate another use of two cameras in the hide.*

During the very brief visit of the cock bird the first exposure was made to obtain a recor but immediately afterwards a better pose was offered and recorded on the other camer Note the difference in depth of focus. The first was taken with 'Luc' shutter at $\frac{1}{80}$ sec. f 16, while for this one the focal plane shutter was used at $\frac{1}{1000}$ sec. at f 3.5.

Pl. 24.

ouse sparrow at feeding-table. An example of bad technique. The large mass of food is
isightly and distracting and the rim of the table is too deep. It might hide a bird's leg.

Meadow pipit feeding young cuckoo. Reflex camera, $\frac{1}{800}$ sec. at f 4.5, 31° Sch. In this
ise the comparatively immobile young bird served to entice the foster parent in front of
our camera.

Pl. 25

Photo. by H. G. Wagsta

Buzzard at rabbit bait. This picture, for which the photographer waited several year
won the first prize in the Bird Section of the British Sporting Exhibition organised
'The Field' at the Imperial Institute in South Kensington.

Pl. 26.

Kyle of Tongue. A typical haunt of waders, especially during migration. A further example of the use of wide angle lens on the miniature camera.

Pl 27.

Dunlins on migration. Photographed with reflex and 12″ telephoto lens.

Sand martins preparing for migration. This type of photograph is possible only with a lo *focus lens and luck.*

Pl. 28.

both these birds, and, perhaps more remarkable still, succeeded in portraying that wary marauder, the carrion crow.

The other possibility in photographing away from the nest is to go to known haunts of the birds. Certain places are much more frequented than others, usually on account of their natural feeding potentialities, and so it is that concentrations of birds are found on sewage farms, river estuaries, and by isolated pools. At these places there is nothing to attract the birds especially to the immediate vicinity of the hide, and so particular care must be taken that the hide is not an object of suspicion, or the chance of even a single photograph will indeed be remote. Birds tend to favour certain parts of a pool or estuary for feeding, and it is advisable to watch them for a little while and then to build the hide in stages in what appears to be a suitable position. Here, again, we recommend that the hide should be of a semi-permanent nature, erected as long in advance of its being used as can be arranged, and, in this particular instance, it should be camouflaged with indigenous material. The photographer must always be escorted to and from the hide by one, or preferably two, assistants.

For this class of work it is not usual to focus on a pre-arranged spot, and so we recommend the use of the reflex camera. It is often possible to focus on the top screen as the subjects are practically all on the ground, and the camera need not be quite at the top of the hide. A telephoto lens is almost essential, and we use the 12-inch Dallon; and as we are working at a much greater range than in the case of photography at the nest, we use the focal plane shutter and find this has little effect on the birds.

Once the photographer is in the hide, and with birds in front of him, the camera must not be moved, except very slowly and quietly; so to facilitate an unobtrusive camera movement, which is of course necessary in this case, and which can be permitted as he is some distance from the birds, he should swing it on the tripod and make provision for the lens to be able to traverse. This is achieved by making, in the front of the hide, an opening about four inches deep and about ten inches long, and screening it by an additional loose curtain hung from above, inside the hide, and fitting closely round the camera lens.

D

Little guidance can be given for the exposures in these circumstances, as the birds will vary enormously in their activity and rapidity of movement, but, in view of the comparatively small depth of focus of the telephoto lenses, it is certainly advisable to give the longest exposure that is consistent with the activity of the birds, and to stop down as far as the light allows.

This class of photography is particlarly interesting and valuable during the periods of migration, and, with a little experience in choosing the most suitable locations for working, it should be possible for anyone to obtain a really good series of records; but this work is, to some extent chancy, and the beginner should not be discouraged if, at his first attempt, the birds all seem so far off. It may be that the hide has been badly sited, but, on the other hand it may just be an unlucky day. The best photographers strike bad patches, but whether they come home at night with many or few exposures to their credit, there is always the satisfaction of what they have seen and learned from their contact with Nature, and even a blank day, photographically, can seldom be counted as without profit.

VIII

The Construction and Use of Special Hides

The 'standard' hides already described serve admirably for the majority of our work, but, from time to time, more elaborate structures have to be built for working in tall trees and other awkward situations. Each case must be treated according to its own peculiar circumstances, but an indication of our method, and a few examples, will assist the beginner in his early attempts.

We endeavour as far as possible to utilize the existing possibilities of the site, and to build our observation platform in the tree in which the nest is built, or in a neighbouring tree or clump of trees; but often this will not allow us to reach the most satisfactory viewpoint, and we have to build tall hides in the required positions.

In anticipation of this work, we take with us on our bird watching expeditions a supply of 6-inch nails and a heavy hammer; a coil of iron wire, about 16 gauge, for lashing those parts of the structure where nails would not hold satisfactorily; about 10 yards of hessian 50 inches wide, for each hide covering, and tacks for fastening it in place; and a good supply of rope for stays, lashings and for hauling equipment up to the hide. A climbing rope is also very useful, and is generally included in our kit.

Let us take, as a first example, the erection of a hide to photograph a kestrel that was nesting in a disused crow's nest high up in a tree. The nest, when discovered, contained four eggs. Incubation had certainly started, but we could not estimate how far it had progressed, except that from the date (it was mid-May), and from the manner of the hen kestrel, we felt that hatching was not far distant. Accordingly, we made our plans, and decided to construct the hide as soon as possible in the hope of having it ready for occupation a little while before the hatch occurred.

The general nature of the task can be seen by referring to plate 29, which shows the nest and the completed hide. The branching habit of the tree made possible the erection of the hide in a position

51

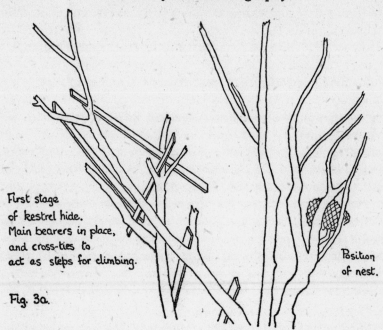

First stage
of kestrel hide.
Main bearers in place,
and cross-ties to
act as steps for climbing.

Position
of nest.

Fig. 3a.

very suitable for photography, except that the nest was rather further from the camera than we should have put it, had we had a choice of positions. A local woodman, who often helped us in this work, quickly surveyed the situation and estimated the amount of timber that would be required, and soon we were on our way to the timber yard on the estate, to see what we could borrow. The agent very kindly fixed us up with several ten foot lengths of 4 by 2-inch joists to act as the main bearers, and a number of 8-inch and 10-inch planks to form the floor. He also supplied some small poles for supporting the walls and roof, and sent the lot on a lorry that happened to be going in the direction of our nest. During that day we concentrated the rest of our tackle in the vicinity, but kept our visits to a minimum in order not to disturb the sitting bird more than was absolutely necessary. For the same reason, no work was done near the kestrel that evening, but the following evening we made a start on the hide.

The main bearers, arranged with their narrow edges at top and bottom so as to give them a 4-inch depth, were fastened in position to form a triangular frame as shown in fig. 3a. Wherever possible, they were supported in a crutch, and in other cases were nailed for extra security. No additional ties or cross-bracing were required to steady this hide, as the whole structure was supported by the branches of one bough only, and these were sufficiently tied by the triangular nature of the main frame. Two stretchers, shown in fig. 3a, were, however, nailed in position below to facilitate the last stages of the climb, and the entry into the hide, which had to be made through the floor. This work was all done in less than half an hour and we then left the neighbourhood as quickly as possible to allow the kestrel to resume her brooding.

Next morning, on our way to another hide, we made a detour to glance at the kestrel to see that all was well. Through binoculars, we could see from a little way off that she was on the nest, so we went away without disturbing her. Our preparations were continued that evening, when we put the floor boards in place, fig. 3b. The two front boards, and the back one, were nailed to the bearers, but two

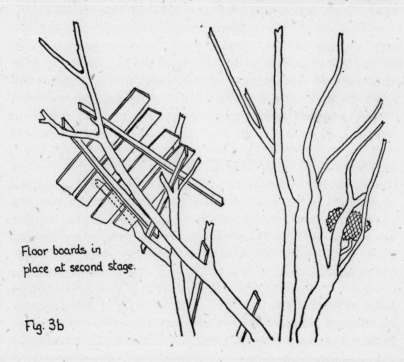

Floor boards in place at second stage.

Fig. 3b

others were left loose so that they could be pushed on top of the fixed boards to provide a way in and out of the hide. This work did not take long, but the placing of the floor boards made the first substantial change in the appearance of the nest environment, so we left it at that, and then left the kestrel for two whole days to accustom herself to the change.

The next move was to erect supports for the walls and roof of the hide. This appeared at first to present some difficulty as there was little to which the uprights could be fixed, but we contrived eventually to fix the left hand front one, which cannot, unfortunately, be seen clearly in the diagram, and then stayed the other two to it, by means of horizontal poles about four feet above the platform. This, again, took about half an hour, and we deemed it advisable to do no more that evening.

The last stage in the construction of the hide was carried out the following evening, when the hessian was fastened to the frame to form the walls and roof. It was stretched as tightly as possible and tacked firmly in place, both to prevent it from blowing about and to increase our sense of security. Hessian may not be very thick or very strong, but it has proved adequate for this purpose, and it is surprising how, if it is securely fastened down, it gives us confidence to work from what would otherwise be a very precarious perch. Before leaving the hide, we made a slit in the front, in the position our camera lens would occupy, and pushed the bottom end of a glass bottle through it to represent the lens. This artifice is desirable in the case of the more wary birds to enable them to get accustomed to the presence of the lens. The bottle was held in place in a horizontal position by a string tied round the neck and fastened to the roof of the hide. All was then ready for photography with the exception of a small amount of 'gardening', but this was left till later, as the offending branch served, for the time being, to screen the hide from the kestrel's gaze and so helped her to disregard it.

On the question of photography, there is little that need be added to what has already been written about photography from the standard hides, but in some instances it will be found desirable to use a lens of greater focal length in order to compensate for the

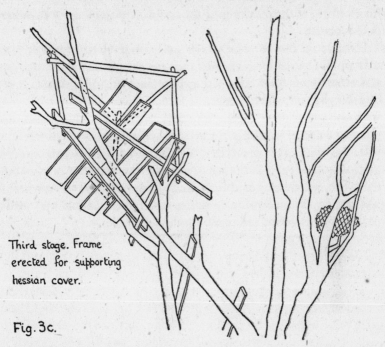

Third stage. Frame
erected for supporting
hessian cover.

Fig. 3c.

increased distance of the camera from the subject. It will, moreover, often be necessary to give shorter exposures, on account of
the camera movement which may occur as a result of the swaying
of the hide.

More often than not, the tree in which the nest is situated will not
provide a suitable perch for the hide, and we have to look round for
other means of supporting the platform. Sometimes this can be
accomplished by using neighbouring trees, as in the case of the
buzzard hide we described in *Intimate Sketches from Bird Life*,
but usually even these seem anywhere but in a good position, and
we are forced to provide our own supports. A typical 'pylon' hide,
as we call this type, is shown in plate 30. The construction will be
self-evident from the photograph, the work being done in stages, as
in the case of the kestrel hide just referred to. Particular features to
notice are, that the poles should be sunk well into the ground to
make the hide stable, and then, if there is any doubt about the
matter, guy ropes should be added. Provision should also be made

for climbing to the platform by the addition of cross strips as shown in the picture.

Finally, we should refer to one particularly useful form of hide that we have used from time to time for the photography of coots and other water-fowl. This is shown in plate 32, and consists simply of a dinghy, on which is mounted a large wooden tripod covered with hessian or other fabric. The device needs no explanation, but just one word of warning. If the dinghy is allowed to float freely, it will sway with every move that we make and will upset the camera adjustment, even if it does not unsettle the birds. It is essential, therefore, whenever possible, to force it into shallow water where it will rest on the bottom, or to wedge it as far as possible with reeds, or with stakes driven into the bottom of the lake.

NEST

The completed kestrel hide, typical of those built in high trees.

Pl. 29.

FLASH-LAMP

NEST

A pylon hide, erected to photograph a tawny owl by flashlight.

Pl. 30.

Flashlight photograph of tawny owl squeezing into nesting hole.

Pl. 31.

Hide erected on dinghy for photographing coots.

Pl. 32.

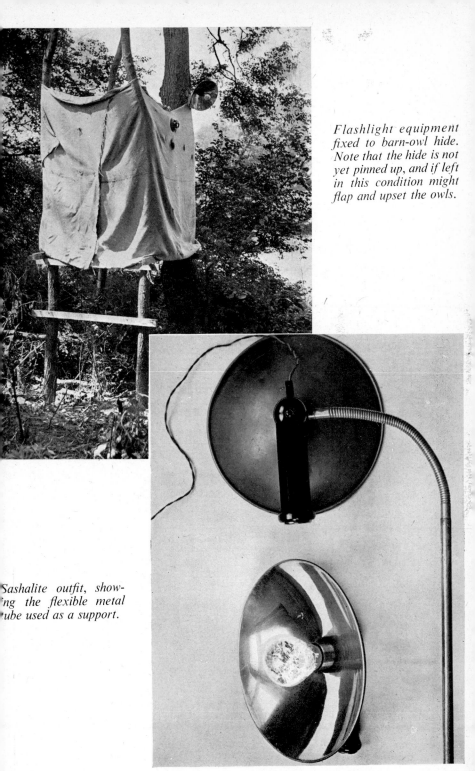

*Flashlight equipment
fixed to barn-owl hide.
Note that the hide is not
yet pinned up, and if left
in this condition might
flap and upset the owls.*

*Sashalite outfit, show-
ing the flexible metal
tube used as a support.*

Pl. 33.

NEST

Long-eared owl hide, similar in construction to a pylon hide but advantage was taken of standing trees to support the platform. Note the board on the right tying the hide to the tree supporting the nest to maintain a constant focal distance.

Pl. 34.

...he long-eared owls which are able to hunt throughout the darkest night. A cock long-
...red owl brings a young rat to the nest while the hen is brooding small chicks. A flash-
...ght photograph taken at night using one large 'Sashalite' bulb at 8 feet from the nest.
$8\frac{1}{2}''$ lens at f 16 with panchromatic film (31° Sch.).

Pl. 35.

Barn owl with a rat in its beak. Flashlight photograph taken at 11.30 p.m.

A pair of barn owls. The male has just given the hen a field vole. Note the owlet shelteri below the hen. A flashlight photograph taken at night in the interior of a barn. Taken w $\frac{1}{4}$ plate field camera. Swing back is used to increase depth of focus. Taylor, Hobson Coo Anastigmat $6\frac{1}{4}''$ Series XI at f 22. 1 Baby Sashalite at 5 ft. on Kodak P.800 plate. Dev oped in D.K.20 for 15 mins. at 68° F.

Pl. 36.

IX

Bird Photography by Flashlight

With the introduction of the modern flash-bulb, the bird photographer has acquired an instrument peculiarly suited to his craft. It extends the range of usefulness of his camera to the world of nocturnal creatures, and improves his prospects of good photography in many a situation where the natural lighting gives little hope of even a mediocre result.

Flash powder is not very suitable for bird photography on account of the noise and smoke it creates, and the danger of fire in dry woodland places. Moreover, it is readily affected by damp, and may fail to ignite at the required time. It is, however, a surprising fact that a flash-bulb, partly perhaps because of the absence of noise or smoke, has practically no disturbing effect on many wild creatures. If very close to the bulb at the instant of firing, they may be momentarily blinded by the flash, but they seem to regard it as some form of natural phenomenon, for they show such indifference to it they they can often be photographed by flashlight several times within a comparatively brief period.

Particularly in view of its potentialities for revealing what the eye cannot see, the flashlight photography of birds is an enthralling pastime, but it is not, as some people seem to imagine, unreasonably difficult. It is, in fact, rather suitable to the circumstances of those whose daily work occupies the major part of the daylight hours, and whose photography during the week must be relegated to the period around sunset.

The camera and equipment that have been used for daylight working serve admirably for flashlight, though we should emphasize the particular advantages of filmpack after dark. It is much easier to handle than plates. The flashlamp is the only additional apparatus required. It consists of a screwed socket to take the flash bulb (an old pocket torch will provide this); a saucer-shaped metal reflector about ten or twelve inches across; a three-volt dry battery to fire the flash-bulb, and about six feet of twin flex with a pear switch on the end; and, of course, a supply of flash bulbs as each can be flashed only once. For those who do not fancy making up this simple apparatus, there are ready-made outfits on the market. One of the best-known of these is the 'Sashalite' outfit illustrated in plate 33. It will be seen that the bulb holder, reflector and battery comprise one unit, the battery being contained in the pistol-grip handle. For remote control, such as is needed in bird photography, there are provided two sockets, into which is plugged the flex leading to the switch.

Our preparations for this branch of photography are generally similar to those already described, except that there is no advantage, and there may often be a disadvantage, in the case of nocturnal creatures, in erecting or adjusting the hide just before dusk. In the case of owls, for example, it is usually best to do this work around mid-day, when the owls are roosting. When the hide is erected, and if possible at least a day before we wish to begin photography, the flash-bulb holder and reflector is fixed in position so that the bird shall have an opportunity to become accustomed to its appearance. We usually fix it to the front of the hide, high up, and displaced as far sideways as possible from the vertical line through the camera lens. A very convenient method of mounting is to attach the flashlight reflector to a length of flexible metal tubing such as is found on some table lamps. This readily allows the direction of the light to be controlled. In practice we attain about three or four feet separation between the camera and the flash-bulb, and find this adequate to provide good modelling in the photograph. We take care, of course, to arrange that the bulb holder is so placed as to be accessible from inside the hide for bulb changing, which is effected by reaching upwards with an arm through a small opening near the top of the hide. Discretion must be used in the matter of fixing the flashlight gear, for while it is desirable to erect it as early as possible, and definitely inadvisable to have to stop to fix it at the time of entering the hide to begin photography, it must be remembered that both the reflector and the battery are liable to deteriorate by undue exposure to the weather.

The camera should be set up if possible during daylight as this not only facilitates focusing, but allows a better inspection of any out-of-focus foreground objects that may have been included in the picture. It is particularly desirable to exclude any twigs or leaves that project towards the flash-bulb, as these would almost certainly be over-exposed, and would result in an unsightly light patch in the finished print. If the camera cannot be set up during daylight, it will be necessary to provide some well-defined and well-illumin- ated object, which can be held close to the nest, and on which focus can be obtained. This can be improvised by superimposing an irregularly shaped piece of opaque paper on a sheet of tissue or other translucent paper, and illuminating it from behind by means of a pocket torch. It is usually insufficient to shine a torch on to the object to be photographed and to try to focus by the reflected light.

Focusing completed, we close the camera shutter and adjust it to the 'bulb' setting, so that it will remain open while the release is pressed, and will close when the pressure is relaxed. We adjust the lens aperture to f22, as this, when used in conjunction with a standard size 'Sashalite' bulb about seven feet from a nest, and with hypersensitive panchromatic film (31° Sch.) loaded into the camera, has been found to give a satisfactory exposure. Alterna- tively the 'Baby Sashalite' bulb may be used in conjunction with a lens aperture of f16 or a little larger.

After making these preparations at the hide, we like, if time permits, to leave the vicinity for a little while, and often take the opportunity to snatch a meal and a hot drink before beginning our spell of watching. Then, about half an hour before dusk, we return to the hide, taking with us a blanket or sleeping bag as suggested in Chapter 7, and sometimes, if the night is very cold, a balaclava helmet. This has slits for the ears in order not to deaden our hearing. The photographer gets inside the hide and settles down, while his assistant tests the circuit to the flash-bulb by inserting a pocket torch bulb in the socket, and watching it for to light when the switch is pressed. If it lights, the circuit is in order, and a 'Sashalite' bulb is inserted. The hide is pinned up at the back, and when the occupant is completely ready for action with shutter release ready to one hand and flashlight switch ready to the other, the assistant takes his leave, making as before, a certain amount of noise to emphasize his departure.

During the early stages of the vigil, while it is still twilight, a certain amount of note taking can be accomplished, but, in the case of most nocturnal birds, the approach to the nest is achieved in almost complete silence, and it is doubly important to keep a sharp look-out for their return. If the night is at all moonlight, we find that sight is the most reliable guide to the correct moment for exposure, but on dark nights, the eyes, after an hour or so of peering into almost utter blackness, can play queer tricks, and we have to work by sound alone. On more than one occasion the occupant of the hide has thought to see, not merely one owl, but several owls return to a nest hole, and has fired a flash, but never yet has the camera recorded what his eyes thought was there and the camera does not lie. Often the only indication of the presence of a bird is the slight scratch of a claw on the bark of the tree, or the 'wheezing' of the chicks as they welcome their parents, but, if care has been taken during the period of twilight to correlate movement with sound, exposures can be timed fairly accurately and a good percentage of successful photographs obtained. In this work, as during daylight, a slight distracting noise, such as a very quiet hiss or squeak, will serve to 'freeze' the bird momentarily, often with the face turned towards the hide, and so will increase the chances of a good photograph, and especially of recording any prey she may carry in her beak.

The method of exposing the film, with the apparatus described, is to press the shutter release at the required moment and to hold it, and immediately afterwards to press the flashlight switch. Pressure on the shutter release is relaxed immediately the flash-bulb has fired. On a really dark night, the shutter may, however, be set at 'Time', and left open for long periods so that only one action, that of pressing the flash-bulb switch, is required at the moment of exposure. In the extremely dilated condition which the eyes assume during the long period of darkness in the hide, they are severely affected by exposure to the flash of the flash-bulb, and temporary blindness lasting one or two minutes may result. This is particularly inconvenient to the photographer as it destroys his chance of following the bird's movements at a time when they are of considerable interest. To overcome this difficulty, we always adopt the expedient of closing one or both eyes during the period of the flash. The object of keeping one eye open is to gain an impression of the bird at the instant of exposure so as to have some idea of the probable photographic result. If, after the flash, that eye is closed and the other one opened and applied to the peep hole, it is often possible to follow the bird's movements and to get some indication of her subsequent whereabouts. This is important as it is most inadvisable to change the flash-bulb while the bird is in the neighbourhood of the nest. The changing should be done as quickly and as quietly as possible as soon as she has left the immediate vicinity.

The procedure for vacating the hide is much the same as described before, but this time our signal for the assistant to approach is a lighted pocket torch dimly glowing in the back of the hide. This stage of the proceedings is generally carried out quite late, often in the small hours of the morning, but certainly during darkness, and, because of a serious accident which entailed the loss of an eye through being attacked by the bird, we strongly recommend the wearing of some form of protection for the face, such as a visor like that used by some motor cyclists, or at least a pair of goggles to pro-

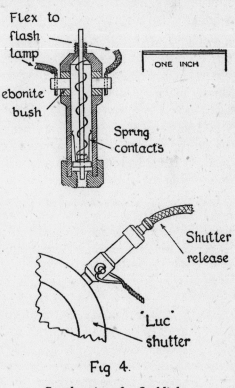

Fig 4.

Synchronizer for flashlight

tect the eyes. More complete protection for the head is given by a fencing mask. This is especially important when working on the tawny owl, which, under cover of darkness will not infrequently attack an intruder near its nest, and, being silent in flight, can approach unperceived. We have, however, noticed that this owl hesitates to attack a person carrying a lighted torch, and we recommend this as an additional precaution when leaving a hide.

Up to this point, flashlight photography has been described only as practised after dark, but we have used it a good deal, and found it very successful to reinforce weak daylight in awkward situations such as dark woods and under shady banks. The only difference in the technique is imposed by the necessity for restricting the period of shutter opening to avoid general fogging of the film. This is achieved by the use of a simple synchronizing mechanism, which, in fact, we devised and made to simplify the procedure at night. The exposure operation, as we described it, is rather clumsy, in that it requires concentration of attention and the use of both hands, but by the use of the little switch device which we illustrate in fig. 4, the operation is reduced to a single pressure with one hand and allows shutter openings, with the 'Luc' shutter, as short as $\frac{1}{30}$th second, with the flash-bulb automatically fired during the exposure interval. It will be noted that with this arrangement, the actual duration of the exposure is controlled by the length of the flash. More elaborate synchronizing devices are available on the market to enable very short exposures to be made within the duration of a flash. These are essential for really high speed work involving rapid wing movement, but their use should be restricted to such occasions as short exposures are not compatible with good depth of focus, and the synchronizers in question cannot be fitted to silent shutters.

X

Birds in Flight

Few natural accomplishments have appealed more to the imagination of man than has the flight of a bird, and yet good photographs of bird flight are comparatively rare. Here then is a subject which challenges the skill of the bird photographer, and will prove itself a fascinating sport as well as a test of photographic ability.

It is quite possible, and in fact necessary, to make plans for this work, but in addition to the programme that is arranged, the photographer will find that a considerable element of luck enters into the scheme of things, and, if he is to make the most of his opportunities, he must be ever ready for a quick action shot as an unexpected subject passes within his range.

From these remarks, it will be obvious that this branch of bird photography has a technique of its own, and that the sturdy field camera that has served so well for other studies, must be replaced by something that can be brought more quickly into use. Here is a field in which the versatile miniature camera is undoubtedly pre-eminent, both on account of its optical properties, and the ease and rapidity with which it can be used.

As mentioned in Chapter IV, we suggest a camera taking 35 mm. film, and equipped with 9 cm. and 13·5 cm. telephoto lenses in addition to the standard 5 cm. lens. Direct vision viewfinders are absolutely essential to enable the camera to be aimed at rapidly moving birds; and range finding and focusing must be capable of quick manipulation. There is no doubt that the ideal arrangement is a combined viewfinder and rangefinder, directly coupled to the lens focusing, but unfortunately this is fitted to very few cameras as yet.

The actual photography of birds in flight can best be considered in two groups as follows:

(a) Long range photography, as instanced by gulls over the water; and

(b) Short range photography, usually from a hide, as for example, the marsh harrier alighting at its nest.

In both cases, a first step to success is to spend some time in watching the particular bird or birds, and in getting to know their habits. Thus, very little association with the buzzard showed her to be persistent in mobbing us as we approached the vicinity of the nest, and we utilized this knowledge to photograph her as she sailed close above us. Similarly, a black-headed gull stooped at us repeatedly every time we traversed a certain dyke. The first time or two it was rather disconcerting; she seemed to swoop so close; but we subsequently took advantage of the performance to record her outstretched wings. At times like these, when the bird acts, more or less, according to form, we can pre-set the focus and concentrate on her flight, exposing when she reaches a predetermined distance. This, to some extent, facilitates the manipulation of the camera, but often we must rely on practice and quick thinking to secure a result. Such a case occurred when a pair of ravens we were watching suddenly mobbed an intruding jackdaw. The whole episode only lasted a fraction of a minute, and was within range for but a few seconds, but the ever-ready miniature came into action and we secured the result shown in plate 40.

For those who must perforce manage flight photography without the help of a miniature camera, we should remind readers of the ¼-plate reflex referred to on page 29. Although not suitable for many rapidly moving subjects, it can be used successfully on some of the larger birds which are comparatively steady in flight, as evidenced by fig. 40, showing the short-eared owl. This was taken with the help of a 12″ telephoto lens.

In work of this kind, exposures, as we have said, must be brief; but even so, with birds travelling at perhaps thirty to forty miles per hour, it is advisable to swing the camera. This is not difficult, but requires a little practice to do it effectively, and we recommend

Short-eared owl and young. Flashlight has been used to give sufficient illumination during late evening.

The dipper in a shady stream. Flashlight used to reinforce daylight.

Pl. 37.

Cock marsh harrier in flight with food held in talons. Short range flight photography.

Cock marsh harrier in flight holding food in bill.

Pl. 38.

Gulls over the water. Long-range flight photography.

The buzzard sailed close above us. Miniature camera, 9 cm., $\frac{1}{200}$ sec., f 5.6, K.1 filter, 31° Sch.

Pl. 39.

*Short-eared owl in flig
An example of a sl
flying bird. Taken with
Reflex camera. 12" Da
telephoto lens at f 5.6.
posure approx. $\frac{1}{1200}$
on Kodak P.1200 pl
Developed in DK.20
15 mins. at 68° F.*

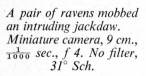

*A pair of ravens mobbed
an intruding jackdaw.
Miniature camera, 9 cm.,
$\frac{1}{1000}$ sec., f 4. No filter,
31° Sch.*

Pl. 40.

the beginner to train his camera on the flight of a few common birds before he sets out in earnest to photograph any special subjects.

Although the photographer is, to so great an extent, an opportunist in the matter of flight photography, he can, in some small measure, control his lighting by being most active when the light is suitable. He should, then, know the conditions that are conducive to the best results. It is our experience that middle-day should be avoided, and that morning or evening gives the best light for the purpose, especially if the camera is facing away from the sun, for at these times the light is soft, and, being from a low-down source, tends to illuminate the under parts of the bird. Moreover, the sky is not unduly bright in the early and late parts of the day, and there is a good chance of rendering a well-toned background with perhaps some cloud pattern. To improve the prospects of this, it is advisable to use a light yellow filter.

With regard to short range flight photography from a hide, there is little that need be added to the camera technique already described, except to emphasize the need for short exposures, a factor which compels the use of either the reflex or the miniature. The focal plane shutter is used on the reflex, and while neither this, nor any of the shutters fitted to the miniatures, are silent, the point does not matter quite so much in the case of photographing birds in flight. In order to achieve success with the brief exposures necessary, it is often desirable to reinforce the natural lighting by means of flashlight, and to synchronize the shutter.

Flight to and from a nest can often be recorded from a hide set up for working as described in chapter VI, the camera being suitably set and focused, and the exposure being made as the bird flies from a nearby perch. A suitable perch should be provided if a natural one is not available. For an actual study in flight, however, it is desirable to record a number of species rather than the one we should have at any one nest, and so we adopt a similar procedure using a feeding table as the centre of attraction.

The method was developed, we believe, by A. J. Speed, who has achieved some remarkable results in this branch of photography. A feeding table some three feet high is established in a situation

x

likely to be frequented by a good variety of birds, and when it has been for some time in use, it is enclosed on three sides and above by wire netting on a wooden frame. The wire should not be too close to the table or it may discourage the birds, but should serve simply to control their direction of approach and departure. If now a suitable perch is erected about four or five feet from the table and rather lower, say about two feet high, it will be found that the vast majority of birds will fly first to the perch, and, after a slight period of hesitation, will fly from there to the table. This provides such a well defined route, that the camera adjustment and focusing can be pre-set and full attention can be given to the instant of exposure. In the case of the small birds, which are somewhat sudden in their movements and quickly off the mark, very quick action will be called for to operate the shutter while they are in flight, but practice, and a little ingenuity in adapting the shutter release to work from a sudden sharp blow rather than from a squeeze of the fingers, will soon enable good results to be obtained with surprising regularity.

XI

Cinematography of Birds

Bird life is so essentially full of movement, so expressive of unbounded vivacity, that our still pictures inevitably fail to convey more than a small part of the charm of birds. The cine camera takes us a stage further. It gives us motion and helps to reveal something of their activity and the fascination of their manner; and even though the cine camera still fails to give the music of bird song, it is a sufficient advance on the work we have described so far to give it an enormous appeal. It is, however, without doubt, the most difficult branch of bird photography, and we do not advise anyone to attempt it until he has had considerable experience of bird watching.

The experience of ordinary bird photography will stand the cinematographer in good stead; but there are fundamental differences between the two branches, the significance of which must be appreciated. In the first place, the image on the cine film is determined once and for always by the position of the camera and the focal length of the lens. It cannot be trimmed to cut out unwanted surroundings, neither can it be controlled locally to reduce, for example, the glare from a shiny leaf, or to add tone to a bald patch of sky. In the second place, the film must be exposed with some reference to a pre-arranged plan, since, to make a satisfactory record, all the different shots must fit together, and must give a properly balanced impression of the features it is desired to portray.

Most of the work will be done from hides, in much the same way as still photography, but, since we are concerned with movement, the hide can often, with advantage, be placed some 30% further from the nest, in order to allow a bigger field of view for a given angular sweep of the camera, and to compensate to some extent for its inevitable purring when in operation. The noise of the cine camera is not, however, as serious as the beginner might expect, and, although most birds will take notice of it at first, they soon disregard it. The hide itself can be similar to those we have already described, but where it is used to support the camera, as in tree-top photography, it should be securely stayed to limit camera movement, which would otherwise cause the image to wander unpleasantly around the screen during projection.

Without doubt, the easiest equipment to use is the standard 35 mm., since very elaborate and comprehensive commercial laboratory facilities are available for this size, and shots can be readily faded in and out, and dissolved into one another, from the editing bench; but the cost of using standard film rules it out of the question for most private photographers. We favour the substandard 16 mm. camera, and have found this very satisfactory in use; and the films, both monochrome and colour, suitable for showing in quite large halls as well as in the home.

As with the still camera, so in this case, a range of interchangeable lenses must be carried, but in cine work it is even more important that the range should be as comprehensive as possible, because from a given position of the hide (and this is often controllable to only a limited extent), we have to rely on the availability of a suitable lens to fill our picture space to the best advantage. In addition to the 1-inch lens, which the photographer is almost certain to need for general purposes, we suggest that he should have a 2-inch and a 3-inch telephoto, and, if funds will allow, a $4\frac{1}{2}$-inch, although this latter will be used much less often than the others.

A photo-electric exposure meter is almost essential, and should be mounted in front of the hide, in such a position that it will give a continuous indication of the light intensity on the subject. We stress this because of the need for matching exposures as closely as possible throughout a cine film. We should, however, utter a word of caution. The exposure meters for cine work are usually designed to have about the same acceptance angle as the normal lens; in our case, the 1-inch. As most of this work will be done with a lens of greater focal length and a smaller acceptance angle, and as the meter cannot be placed forward to register the same field as the camera lens, we must watch our subject carefully, and, if necessary, make whatever allowances seem indicated.

Turning now to the procedure in the hide, we suggest that the first thing the photographer should do is to study his particular quarry for a little while before starting to use the cine camera. It is important to prepare, beforehand, an outline plan of the intended film, and this demands, on the part of the photographer, both a general understanding of the species, and an acquaintance with the habits of the particular bird being photographed. Without this knowledge, the only result of the filming would be a series of unrelated episodes, and what is more, only a very small percentage of the film used would be of any value at all. Anyone with the slightest experience of bird watching will appreciate this, the more so if he has seen, for example, the slow and cautious approach of a peewit to her nest, or the deliberate and protracted behaviour during the hatching of a brood of young partridges. It is necessary, in making a cine film, to contract into a short space what in fact takes a considerable time; and to do it without giving a false impression of the time scale. It can be done only by careful planning, by knowing in advance the main shots that will be taken, and working in between these a succession of different, but related shots, that will give continuity, and, at the same time, will, by their interruption of the main shots, suggest the passage of time.

While this preliminary study of the bird is taking place, the photographer can be taming it to ignore the noise of the camera. He should begin cautiously, and, as in the case of still photography, allow it to return at first without any disturbance. When it is comfortably settled, he can run the camera for a short while, the camera being not yet loaded, but should be ready to stop at the first sign of uneasiness on the part of the bird. He may find that it will cock its head and listen at first, but that is natural and is nothing to worry about; but at the first suggestion of movement, he should stop, and let the bird settle again. The next time, it will probably be less attentive to the camera, and subsequently will hardly notice it. Then the camera should be loaded with film, and photography begun.

It occurs to us that readers may be interested to know something of our experiences in making bird films, and as a recent example will be appearing in the cinemas at about the time this book is published, we cannot do better than choose that as our subject. We refer to the actual bird shots from the film *Tawny Pipit*. This was produced by Two Cities Films and we had, in consequence, the advantage of being able to select from a wide range of apparatus that was put at our disposal. We also had the inestimable help of that well-known cameraman, Eric Cross. Two cameras were used. There was a Newman-Sinclair with 40 mm., 50 mm., 75 mm., and 100 mm., and 6″, 8″ and 16″ lenses for filming the birds at the nest, and an Imo camera with 2″, 4″ and 6″ lenses for filming them in flight. The N-S with its wide range of lenses allowed us to take general views of the nest surroundings or close-ups in which the nest itself filled the whole picture space, with any desired proportion between these extremes.

Having found a suitable nest, we erected two hides and worked them up into position as explained in Chapter V. They were left in their final positions for a whole day before they were used, and by that time the birds were well accustomed to them, and appeared to be behaving quite naturally, but we found, as we usually have in such cases of bird cinematography, that the birds were a little upset by the noise of the camera when they first heard it. Taming proceeded as already described and the birds were very soon perfect subjects for the camera. The 75 mm. lens was the one we used most, but the 100 mm. and the 8″ were close runners-up, the latter being used for most of the close-ups. Shots were taken of the bird running on to the nest, settling down to brood the eggs, feeding the young, and in fact of almost all the activities that go to make up life at the nest. The important point, that will be noted by those bird photographers who see the film, is that the subject was shot from many different angles. The frequent changes of camera position involved in this procedure led us, in this case, to adopt a slightly different procedure from the normal, but one which is worth recording as it may be of use in other instances. Due largely to the fact that the view finder was awkwardly placed for looking out of the hide, together with the fact that the camera and tripod were large and heavy for manipulating in confined quarters, we found it easier and quicker when setting up the camera to dismantle the hide, erect and focus the camera, and then re-erect the hide over the camera. This took very little time and in no way upset the birds and we commend it as an alternative procedure in the case of cinematography with large equipment.

It is difficult to suggest a typical scheme for a film, as there is essentially so much variation from one to another, both in purpose and subject, but a few general hints may not be out of place. Having completed our preliminary observations, we jot down a list of the key shots that are essential to our plan, paying particular attention to the continuity of idea, and then tick these off as each is filmed. The shots will not, in general, be filmed in the order in which they are to appear in the final production, but, by working to a plan, we avoid having awkward gaps in the finished story.

Although we recommend this system of careful preparation for cinematography, the photographer will, in practice, be confronted with unexpected events, just as much as in any other branch of bird watching, and it would, of course, be stupid to miss opportunities of recording anything of value or special interest, simply because it was not included in the original plan. He must, therefore, be always on the alert to modify his working in the light of experience, though, at the first opportunity, the skeleton plan should be rebuilt to ensure a coherent result.

The actual photographic technique follows closely that referred to in Chapter VI, with just the usual modifications that apply to the cine camera, and, with that in mind, we cannot do better than refer the cinematographer to this, and then leave him to evolve his plans, and to develop them as a result of experience.

XII

Trees, Flowers and Insects

The infinite variety of Nature is one of her greatest charms, but such is the profusion of form and colour, and such is the abundance of species, that few men or women can profess to have a detailed knowledge of more than a limited range of natural history. Most of us tend to specialize to some extent, but whether our main interest lies in fishes or fungi, mosses or moths, or in some other limited sphere, it is certain that we could not, even if we wished, ignore the rest of the realm of Nature. Life of all forms is so inter-dependent that a study of one form brings us immediately into touch with several others, and our interest, while still centred on one subject, tends to widen.

So it is with bird watchers; and while their particular study, because of the mobility of birds, has connections with almost every branch of natural history, the three subjects which form the heading of this chapter have perhaps a special attraction for them, as they provide the greater part of the food and shelter of the birds that live on land. Even apart from their avian associations, these subjects make a special appeal to photographers, and there can be few who at some time or other have not wanted to record the beauty of form of a well-grown tree, or the marvellous detail and workmanship in the structure of a wasps' nest.

The subjects of this chapter can all be photographed with the field camera that was used in the hide, but it should preferably be fitted with a lens of about 6-inch focal length, or the bellows extension will be undesirably long in the case of close-up objects. There is, however, a drawback to the use of this camera, in that it takes rather a long time to erect and adjust, and this counts particularly when most of the work consists of casual shots by the wayside.

Note: 'Flower' in this chapter, may mean a flowering plant, or an individual blossom or cluster of blossoms, or both, according to the context.

Flowers and insects can also be recorded by the miniature, but this camera is not so suitable for trees on account of the lack of a rising front.

We prefer, therefore, to carry a special camera for most of this work. It is a 3½-inch by 2½-inch folding plate camera having double extension bellows, and a rising and cross motion for the lens mount. The lens is of 10·5 cm. (about 4¼ inch) focal length and has a maximum aperture of f4·5. The shutter has a wide range of speeds, but the important ones are the slow speeds of $\frac{1}{10}$, $\frac{1}{5}$, $\frac{1}{2}$ and 1 second. With the camera, we carry a small metal telescopic tripod fitted with a universal joint head, a pale yellow filter, and a stock of panchromatic plates, usually Ilford Soft Gradation, or Kodak P. 500. Film pack is carried as a reserve, in case a large number of subjects are encountered during one outing. We also usually carry a number of accessories for the preparation and arrangement of specimens in the field, but details of these are best left until they are referred to later in connection with their special uses.

Trees

Perhaps the two most important things to consider in the photography of trees are (1) the choice of specimens and (2) the weather and lighting conditions. The best rendering is achieved only when the tree, or group of trees, stands out clearly from its surroundings. This does not always mean that an isolated specimen must be found, especially as in some cases, as for instance the hazel, this would give a false impression of the typical habitat; but what it does mean is that the tree must be at least sufficiently prominent among its neighbours for a viewpoint to be chosen such that its form is clearly shown.

The photography of trees should, if possible, be undertaken on days of light fleecy or broken cloud and only slight wind, a period of sunshine being chosen for the actual instant of exposure. When the best viewpoint has been selected, the photographer should note the position of the sun, and if this is not suitable, that is, well behind the camera, he should estimate the best time of day for his purpose, and, if possible, return when conditions are most favourable. The camera should be erected on the tripod and focused, using the ground glass screen, care being taken to see that the screen is truly vertical, as otherwise the tree may appear to be leaning backwards in the final picture. If, with the screen vertical, the top of the tree cannot be included in the picture space, the rising front should be used to raise the lens in relation to the film.

We generally use the yellow filter when working on trees, especially if there are cloud formations we want to include in our picture, and we keep exposures slightly on the full side with a view to subsequent soft development. The actual shutter speed used must depend chiefly on the amount of movement of the tree, but we like to work at speeds of about $\frac{1}{2}$ to 1 second, when possible, and to stop down the lens to suit this and the prevailing light intensity. The resulting small aperture then assists in the attainment of good definition of the fine tracery of twigs and foliage. On occasions, especially when photographing at short range a shrub or small tree that is rather confused with its background, it is desirable to use a large stop to throw the background out of focus and to concentrate the definition and, in consequence, the interest, on the principal subject. The shutter speed must in that case be adjusted to suit the lens aperture. There can be no hard and fast rule as to which technique should be adopted, but, with very little experience, the photographer will be able to assess the needs of any particular situation.

The mere taking of a single tree photograph is not of particular interest unless the tree has some unique feature, or unless it composes well to yield a print of pictorial merit, but tree photography acquires more interest and value if it is pursued with a definite purpose. This may be to record specimen trees in a given locality, or to illustrate a life cycle with pictures of a sapling, and the full grown tree in summer and in winter. In addition, detail photographs may be taken of the bole and the leaf, the male and female flower, and the seed; and, to trespass for a moment into the realm of insects, we may wish to illustrate the common pests and diseases to which the tree is subject. Some of these details are best treated as individual specimens cut from the tree and arranged in front of an artificial background, but this technique will be described in a separate section later in this chapter.

Flowers

Although much of the attraction of a flower lies in its colour, a good photograph in monochrome is an excellent means of illustrating its structure and habitat, and, if skilfully taken, may convey at least a suggestion of its delicacy and beauty.

In the photography of a wild flower *in situ*, the choice of specimen is of supreme importance, and with the selection of a well-placed subject the photographer's difficulties are more than half over. This question must be considered carefully, because, in Nature, many flowers are more or less hidden and confused amongst a tangle of grasses and other vegetation, and in such conditions even the most perfect photographs could not give clear indications of the subject. Extensive removal of the unwanted material must not be undertaken because plants are very greatly affected by their immediate environment. Their growth may be stunted, or forced and spindly, according to whether they have been in an exposed situation, or smothered among other plants, so that, to achieve a satisfactory photograph, the exposure must be made on a subject that has been disturbed as little as possible. If resort were had to drastic clearing, the result would be not only very unnatural, but also, in most cases, very unsightly, as a result of the bare and possibly blanched stems that had been exposed. The ideal subject for a flower study is one that is a normal specimen, and, without being in a freak situation, is boldly placed in relation to its surroundings.

The viewpoint must, of course, be considered at the same time as the subject is selected. Except in the case of very tall flowers, the camera should be tilted slightly downwards to give a natural aspect. It should not be held directly over the flower, as this would dwarf the plant and fail to show its habit; neither should it, in general, be placed so low as to give an unnatural under-side view. The direction from which the photograph is taken will depend only a little on the relative position of the sun, since a soft lighting is usually essential for this work and the moment of exposure should be deferred, if necessary, until the sun is obscured. The viewpoint should also be chosen so that the background is as plain as possible; that is, free from awkward shaped masses or a confusing tangle of undergrowth. It is often possible, especially in the case of plants, such as meadowsweet, growing on the side of a mound or on a river bank, to choose the viewpoint so that the plant is seen against a distant background, and where this is possible, advantage should be taken of the fact, and a large stop used to throw the background out of focus.

If on occasions flowers must be photographed at a time when there is no prospect of cloud obscuring the sun, we shade the subject of the photograph with our focusing cloth; but in doing this we take care that the cloth is neither too close, in which case it would give a 'dead' lighting, nor yet too far away so that the shade does not cover the whole of the camera field. It may be necessary, when using this artifice, to tilt the camera rather more than would otherwise be desirable, in order to cut off from the picture some of the background which is beyond the limit that we can shade.

It is our experience that the photography of wild flowers tries the patience a good deal more than the photography of birds, for the perfect flower study frequently demands a nice balance of conditions which it is beyond the power of the photographer to control, but for which he should be prepared to wait. The instant of exposure is seldom governed, as in the case of bird photography, by particular and perhaps unique action on the part of his subject, and he has, in consequence, little excuse for not waiting for at least good, if not perfect, conditions. Although, as we have stated, the light must not be strong, neither must it be very dull, for even on the calmest of days there is a surprising amount of movement among the flowers and grasses, and long exposures are often quite out of the question. In the case of dwarf plants, such as the violet, where the movement is only spasmodic, occurring with wind gusts and eddies, moderately long exposures may perhaps be given, the safe duration of which must be judged by watching the particular plant for a little while before taking the photograph. This is fortunate, for it is usually this type of plant that cannot be viewed against a distant background, and, to avoid a severe and rapid deterioration of definition across the picture, as small a stop as possible must be used to get good depth of focus. Tall, slender flowers, such as campion or ragged robin, seem to sway continuously, and exposures must usually be $\frac{1}{10}$th second or less, but it is such subjects that allow most frequently the use of large stops, giving a well-defined subject against a completely out-of-focus background. Where such an arrangement is not possible, or where the wind is unduly troublesome, some benefit can often be obtained by screening the flower from the wind, and for this purpose the focusing cloth is again useful.

There are some flowers, as for instance the bluebell, which are particularly attractive to the eye when in large drifts. Much of this attraction lies in the expanse of colour, and we would warn, beginners especially, against attempting to record this in monochrome. The result would be disappointing because it would show neither the colour, nor the form, of the flower. When working in monochrome, it is best to concentrate on form and texture, and so the best results are obtained by confining the attention to a single flower or a small cluster.

Insects

There are so many species of insects, and they have such widely varying characteristics, that nothing short of a complete volume could deal adequately with the subject of recording them by photographic means. We shall, however, try here, by means of a few generalizations, to indicate how bird photographers can add to the interest of their records by including a few of the more common insects they encounter in the field.

Some moths may be found asleep on walls and fences during daylight, and as in many instances they provide an excellent illustration of camouflage through colour harmonization, they should be photographed without being disturbed.

A more certain way of photographing moths, however, is to work after dark, attracting the moths to a few selected tree trunks by means of a bait, made up as follows. Black treacle and some beer dregs are boiled together, and to every four parts of the mixture, one part of brown sugar is added. This bait keeps well in a sealed jar, but before starting out on an expedition, a little rum should be added to freshen it, and render it more potent. Towards dusk, the mixture is painted on a few trees, here and there, at a convenient height, say about three feet from the ground, and within a short time quite a few moths will have settled to feed.

We select a specimen, and, since subsequent identification of a moth from a monochrome photograph is often difficult, identify it on the spot by reference to a handbook on moths. Good books for the purpose are either, *Moths of the British Isles*, by Richard South, or *Butterflies and Moths*, by W. E. Kirby. Then, with camera erected on tripod, we focus as best we can. In the case of these comparatively small subjects it is usually possible to illuminate them sufficiently with a good pocket torch, but we find a focusing magnifier of great assistance for this work.

Exposure is, of course, by artificial light, and although magnesium ribbon could be used, we prefer to use a 'Baby Sasha-lite' bulb. This, fired at about three feet from the moth, allows the lens to be stopped down to about f22, provided panchromatic plates such as Kodak P.1200 are employed.

Butterflies are an attractive subject and can be dealt with in daylight. In fact, they feed most during sunshine. Many of them are rather timid and difficult to approach in the ordinary way, but they, too, can be bribed to pose. The usual expedient is to select a suitable flower (preferably one by itself, although if others intrude into the picture they can be removed), and to focus the camera on to it. The flower is then baited with a small spot of honey, which proves an irresistible attraction to any passing butterfly, and holds its attention, so that exposures of $\frac{1}{5}$ to $\frac{1}{2}$ second can often be given, and the lens aperture made correspondingly small. Other insects, for example bees and wasps, can be encouraged to remain for a little while in one place by similar offerings, but care must be taken in the matter of exposure since some of them are relatively active.

A great number of the insects that we encounter are rather too small to be photographed in the ordinary way, but can be recorded very well if they are magnified. This is an interesting branch of the subject and can be followed with very little addition to the equipment that has already been described. The essential thing is to have a camera which has a long bellows extension and to fit it with a lens of short focal length. The field camera serves admirably for this purpose, and we use it with a 1-inch lens, which at some time or other did duty in a cine camera. It gives good results up to magnifications of about 15 diameters, which is ample for a very large amount of work.

In photomicrography of this kind, we have, inevitably, a rather small depth of focus, and so must usually stop down well to get satisfactory results. This means long exposures if we rely on natural lighting, and so, for subjects which show much movement, we again resort to flashlight, firing a standard Sashalite bulb about two feet from the subject. It is often possible, and in such cases is advantageous, to bring the specimen indoors to be photographed. This demands much less patience, as more control can be exercised over both the subject and the lighting. The former can often be restrained in a small enclosure having plate glass at the front and back, and the light can be provided by two Photoflood bulbs, placed one to each side, and about two feet away. The exposure must be ascertained by trial as it is dependent on the camera extension; that is, the magnification. In all these instances of photomicrography, the best method of focusing is to rack out the camera lens until it gives about the degree of magnification required, and then to achieve the final sharp focus by moving the whole camera to or from the subject, or the subject to or from the camera, whichever is the more convenient.

Posed Specimens

From time to time we wish to photograph specimens of flowers, seeds, leaves, and other similar objects, and yet cannot conveniently take the photograph *in situ*. In such cases we have to collect the required specimens, and either remove them to a more convenient position in the field, or take them home to be dealt with.

The principle item needed, after the photographic equipment already described, is a suitable plain background about 24 inches long by about 20 inches high. This sounds rather an awkward thing to carry about, but it can be made easily portable by constructing it of a piece of fabric fastened at each end to a stick similar to a broom handle. The sticks should be about 24 inches long so that they project 4 inches below the bottom of the screen and can be pushed into the ground to hold the screen erect. When not in use, the screen is rolled round one of the sticks and is kept fastened by a length of tape tied round the bundle. It is an advantage if the screen is made of double thickness with two different materials, so that one side is black or dark coloured, and the other is a light grey. The material should not be glossy.

Other minor, but useful, items of equipment comprise several lengths of string, a wooden stick about 18 inches long with a 'bulldog' paper clip fastened to one end, and a few ordinary pins.

A walnut twig will serve excellently as an example of 'posing'. In its growing position on the tree it would have been awkward to photograph, both on account of its inaccessibility, and the continual movement, but as a 'posed' subject, it is simplicity itself. The first, and a most important, requirement is to note carefully the orientation of the twig. That is to say, notice which side is uppermost and whether the twig has a rising or a drooping tendency. Only after this has been done should the twig be cut. It is then taken to the place chosen for photography, which should be a spot sheltered from the wind, and where the light is good, but diffused. A brief look at the specimen held near the background cloth will show whether the light or dark side is the more suitable, and the background is then erected with the chosen surface facing the prevailing direction of the light. The specimen is usually supported in a natural attitude, a few inches in front of the background, and is held in place by the 'bulldog' clip, the stick supporting which is pushed into the ground. In some cases, however, the subject is more conveniently, and without detriment to the photograph, laid directly on the background cloth, which is spread on the ground.

A little experience will soon show the possibilities of this class of work, both as regards the range of subjects and the methods of dealing with them. The hints that have been given serve as but an indication of what can be done, and we must leave the reader to fill in many gaps and develop the details of his own technique.

The beauty of form of a well-grown white poplar. The selection of subject is an important part of tree photography.

Pl. 41

Walnut in winter.

Pl. 42.

Walnut in summer.

Pl. 43.

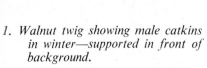

1. *Walnut twig showing male catkins in winter—supported in front of background.*

2. *Male catkins and female flowers of a walnut in summer.*

3. *Fruit of walnut.*

4. *Walnut bole.*

5. *Walnut leaf laid flat on light background.*

Pl. 44.

Bluebells. We confine our attention to a small cluster.

Hemlock water dropwort. The focusing cloth was used to cut out an awkward natural background.

Wall pennywort. A flower study boldly placed in relation to its surroundings.

Meadow sweet. Photographed against a distant out-of-focus background.

Pl. 45.

Ladybird (Halyzia 16 guttata). Low power photo-micrograph.

Puss Moth asleep in situ. 3½" × 2½" folding camera. 10.5 cm. Zeiss Tessar lens at f 22. Exposure 2 secs. on Ilford HP.2 plate in poor daylight.

Pl. 46.

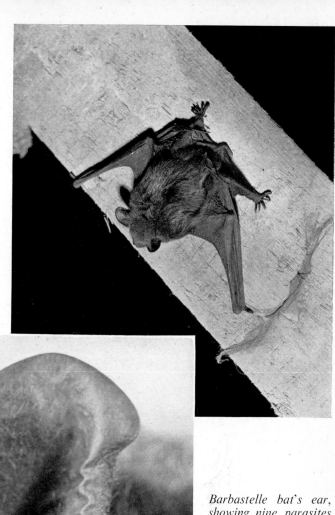

The serotine bat at rest. This large species whose wing-span often reaches 14 ins. or more, should be looked for in Southern England. Taken with a ¼-plate field camera. 8½″ Serrac lens at f 16. 1 Baby Sashalite bulb at 3 ft. from subject. Ilford Soft Grad. Pan. Plate. Developed in DK.20 for 18 mins. at 68° F.

Barbastelle bat's ear, showing nine parasites (of the family Acarina) along the outer margin. The spear-shaped skin-formation resembling an inner ear is known as the tragus. Low Power Photomicrograph (× 7). Taken with ¼-plate field camera. T.-H. Cooke 6¼″ Series XI at f 8. 3 sec. exposure with Photoflood lamp on Ilford Soft Grad. Pan. plate.

Pl. 47.

Capercaillie photographed in intense sunlight, yet detail retained in shadow by over-exposure and curtailed development.

Ptarmigan nest and eggs. An example of the fine grain that can be obtained with D.K. *developer. Negative on 35 mm. film.*

Pl. 48.

XIII

Nature in Colour

Colour is one of Nature's greatest charms and every photographer faced with the task of portraying the splendour of a colourful bird or flower, or the more subtle tones of a peaceful landscape, must at some time or another have exclaimed, 'Oh, if only I could take that in colour!'

Colour photography has been a practical possibility for many years now; a volume which we have to hand, dated 1904, gives details of the Lumière process and reveals it as essentially the same as we know it today; but it is only recently that colour photography has been at all generally practised, and even yet there is no successful popular method of producing colour prints available in this country, though the technical difficulties have been to some extent solved and a process is available in the United States, and will be here soon after the war.

For the present, then, we must be content to see our colour photographs as transparencies; to look at them through a viewer, or to project them on to a screen: but such is the fascination of colour that this inconvenience is well worth while, and the results amply repay the little extra trouble that is needed to obtain them.

Before turning our attention to the processes and equipment available, let us consider for a moment the general peculiarities and problems associated with colour photography. First, the fastest colour films available are slower than the monochrome films that are generally used for Nature subjects. This means that, since exposures cannot usually be increased on account of movement of the subject, we must either work in a better light or use a larger lens aperture. The latter would lead to a reduction in the depth of focus and cannot usually be tolerated, since out of focus backgrounds are much more objectionable in a colour picture than in black and white, because the contrasts created by the colours themselves prevent a merging to a uniform or unobtrusive background pattern.

Thus, for the attainment of the best colour photographs of moving subjects, we must limit our activities to periods of good lighting, which often means sunshine. From one point of view this is no disadvantage, for the sun helps to bring out the brilliance of colour in most subjects. Furthermore, the response of colour films is adjusted in manufacture to give a correct colour rendering when exposed in lighting approximating to noon summer sunshine.

Exposure in strong sun, however, raises another problem, for, as we saw in Chapter VI, nature subjects are frequently of such high contrast that direct sunlight should be avoided even when they are photographed in monochrome, and colour films have still less latitude. We are obliged then to compromise. We need sunshine to provide the level of illumination desirable for Nature photography in colour, and to give brilliance to our pictures; but we must avoid excessive contrasts in our subject, otherwise correct exposure for the middle tones will lead to over-exposure of the highlights and under-exposure of the shadows, with consequent false colours in those parts of the picture. This compromise is best effected by making the exposure when the sun is lightly veiled by thin cloud and by working with the sun as nearly as possible behind the camera. We have even made very successful colour transparencies of birds and flowers in strong sunshine by taking extra care to reduce the shadow areas of the picture to an absolute minimum. This is achieved by arranging the camera exactly between the sun and the subject and then moving the camera the least distance downwards or sideways so that the shadow of the camera is not included in the field of view. No fear need be entertained that this flat lighting will result in a lack of modelling, for the colour itself gives rise to a modelling which is even more effective than the shadow modelling of a monochrome picture.

There is another useful technique which we have successfully employed on days of alternating cloud and sunshine. It consists of giving two exposures on the same piece of film: one when the sun is obscured and the other when it is shining. The camera must, of course, be rigidly supported so that it cannot move between the two exposures but otherwise there is no difficulty in the method when dealing with static subjects. We usually calculate the exposure for the cloudy condition and then expose for about 80% of the calculated value. Then, when the sun comes out we make the other exposure, giving about $\frac{1}{4}$ to $\frac{1}{10}$th (depending on the brilliance of the sun) of the exposure that we gave previously. By this technique we can, even in contrasty subjects, get adequate exposure in the shadows and yet benefit from that glint of brilliance that the sunshine gives to the highlights. We should mention that a slight difficulty arises when using a camera which has the film-winding mechanism geared to the shutter setting, but this can be overcome by opening the camera shutter on the 'time' setting and then using the lens cap, or another shutter fitted in front of the lens, to make the exposures.

It need hardly be remarked that the comparatively small latitude of colour film means that exposures must be particularly accurate, and a photo-electric exposure meter is almost indispensible. Moreover, since meters vary somewhat between themselves it is advisable for each photographer to make a test with his own meter. To do this a day should be chosen when the light is reasonably steady. A meter reading should be taken of a suitable stationary subject and an exposure made, using the film manufacturer's rated speed. Other exposures should then be made on the same subject, giving, in turn, half a stop smaller, and then a whole stop smaller; and half a stop larger and a whole stop larger, making five exposures, all at the same shutter speed. It is advisable to include some identification, such as a numbered card, in the field of view each time so that the different exposures can be readily recognized. If from this test it is found that the exposure at a stop larger than the first one gives the best result, it means that for that particular meter the film should be rated 3° Sch. less than the manufacturer's rating or, if the smaller stop wins, the film can be rated faster. The great thing is to get to know the film and the meter; to keep them working together as a team; and to recognize their limitations.

In a short chapter such as this it is not possible to give full details of all the colour processes available, but we can outline the main types and indicate their advantages and disadvantages from the point of view of bird and other nature photography. The earlier processes derived their colour from a mosaic of minute coloured starch grains which formed a layer in front of the photographic emulsion and so acted as filters though which the photograph was taken and then, after processing, acted as filters through which the transparency was viewed. Variations of this process use finely ruled colour screens to form a 'reseau' to give the same effect. Examples of such processes are Lumiere, Finlay and Dufay. More recently a method has been developed by which dye images are generated in the emulsion at the time of development of the photographic image. This method is represented by Kodachrome and Agfa-colour.

All the processes give reasonably good colour reproduction, the early Lumière process being as good as any from this point of view, but there are marked differences between the processes in the matter of transparency and hence luminosity of image. It is in this respect that the later process scores heavily, for, in the course of processing, all the silver grains are dissolved away, leaving a clear dyed gelatine image. This feature also results in a complete absence of grain and consequently permits the attainment of remarkably fine definition.

Our own leaning is towards Kodachrome for its brilliance of image combined with good colour rendering, but a drawback to the use of this by the enthusiastic photographer is that it cannot be processed at home and in consequence some of the photographic interest is lost. Furthermore, results cannot be so quickly available with this as they could be with home processed material. Where it is important to have a result quickly we turn to Dufay and process it ourselves following the method given in the Dufay handbook. Commercial processing of Dufay is available if required. While this process gives good colour rendering, the transparencies are inevitably more dense than Kodachromes because of the presence of the silver image, and they tend to be less satisfactory for lantern projection of this account.

As we have already emphasized, adequate depth of focus is difficult to attain in the photography of close-up subjects such as birds and flowers in colour, so we must utilize every factor that will help in this direction. For this reason the miniature camera with its short focus lens is often to be preferred to the larger sizes we have advocated for monochrome photography. Moreover, in the case of a transparency for projection, the small size is very little disadvantage, especially with the Kodachrome process, for the fine definition possible in the dye image can stand considerable enlargement with little loss of quality. Even so, in those cases where long exposures can be given and the lens aperture correspondingly reduced to give us good depth of focus, we unhesitatingly recommend a larger size, though for the preparation of lantern slides there is no point in going above $3\frac{1}{2}'' \times 2\frac{1}{2}''$.

During the war, very little colour film is available for general use, but prior to the restriction on supplies, Dufay was available as roll film and film pack for most of the popular sizes and was also made up in cassettes for 35 mm. miniature cameras and 16 mm. cine film. Presumably all these will be available again when times are more normal. Kodachrome has so far been generally available in this country only for 35 mm. and 40 mm. × 28 mm. miniature cameras and for 16 mm. and 8 mm. cine cameras, but larger sizes are available in the United States and should be here before long; and having been privileged to use a little of this material already, we can say with assurance that it is worth looking forward to, and should give a great boost to popular colour photography.

XIV

Darkroom Notes

It is not intended in this chapter to give complete instruction in the development of negatives and the making of prints, but rather to emphasize to the photographer, already familiar with these processes, the special requirements of bird photography.

In the first place, we urge that negatives should be developed very soon after they have been exposed, in order that, should the unexpected have happened, and a series of blanks have resulted, there may yet be an opportunity to repeat some of the exposures. We cannot forget the unfortunate experience of a friend of ours, who on developing some three hundred negatives taken during a holiday spent in bird photography, found that, as a result of a defect in his camera, every photograph was badly fogged. The work involved in the erection of the hide and in other preparations are such that any simple precaution that will avoid the risk of total failure is fully justified.

Those photographers who are working intermittently and from their own homes as bases, should find little difficulty in keeping up to date with the development of negatives, but it is during periods away from home that the extra effort is needed to secure rapid checking of results. Before starting work in a fresh district we endeavour to ascertain the local facilities for development of films, and then take with us everything necessary to complete the task. Sometimes arrangements may be made with a local photographer for the occasional use of his darkroom, but in other cases we do all our development in the house where we are staying. This is not unduly difficult as a rule, as the negatives are always developed by time and temperature, and the only darkness needed is for loading the film, after exposure, into the light-tight tank.

Perhaps the greatest difficulty in developing negatives away from home lies in the matter of transporting the necessary equipment, although if a car is not available, it can be packed amongst clothing in a trunk and sent by rail in advance. The minimum equipment required consists of the developing tank (or tanks, if more than one size is used); an enamel jug with a capacity equal to that of the tank; bottles and chemicals for developing and fixing solutions, about which more will be discussed later; a funnel, and some cotton wool; a thermometer, a plate rack, and clips for hanging up the film negatives to dry; and finally, some transparent envelopes or other means of storing the finished negatives. In cases where no water supply or sink is readily available, we need a couple of large buckets, but these can generally be borrowed locally. In some places the water may contain an appreciable amount of suspended solid matter, and to be prepared for this, it is as well to have some pieces of washed muslin to use as filters.

It is a good plan to prepare the developer and fixer before photography is begun, and to keep them in tightly corked bottles, as this reduces the risk of undissolved particles at the time of development. For development of ¼ plate and 3½ by 2½-inch negatives, we make up the Ilford 1D.2. formula, dissolving the ingredients in the following order:

Metol - - - - - -	20 grains
Sodium sulphite (crystals) - -	3 ozs.
Hydroquinone - - - -	80 grains
Sodium Carbonate (crystals)' - -	2 ozs.
Potassium Bromide - - -	20 grains
Distilled Water (warm) to make -	20 ozs.

This is a concentrated stock solution and so is not too bulky for our purpose, a 20-oz. bottle being sufficient to develop about four ¼-plate film packs or about six of the smaller size.

In addition to the above developer,[1] we prepare a 20-oz. bottle of special developer for the miniature films. This is a fine grain

[1] Since writing this, we have tended to dispense with 1D.2. and to use the fine grain developer for the majority of large negatives as well as for the miniature negatives. It gives very satisfactory results, and it is often convenient to be able to manage with only one developer when away from home. This is not, however, in accordance with the manufacturer's recommendations, and so we retain the 1D.2. formula in the book for those who prefer to use it.

developer devised by Kodak and known as DK.20. The formula is as follows:

> Distilled Water (at about 125° F) - 15 ozs.
> Metol - - - - - 44 grains
> Sodium Sulphite (crystals) - - 4 ozs.
> Kodalk - - - - - - 17½ grains
> Potassium Thiocyanate - - - 9 grains
> Potassium Bromide - - - 4½ grains
> Make up with cold distilled water to 20 ozs.

This developer is used at the strength given above, but even so, it makes no great demands on storage or transport space as it may be used repeatedly, provided it is kept in a well-corked bottle. Its strength is maintained practically constant by re-bottling only 19¼ ozs. each time after use, and adding to it ¾ oz.[1] of the following replenisher to restore the full volume of 20 ozs.

> Distilled Water (at about 125° F) - 15 ozs.
> Metol - - - - - - 66 grains
> Sodium sulphite (crystals) - - 4 ozs.
> Kodalk - - - - - - 175 grains
> Potassium Thiocyanate - - - 44 grains
> Potassium Bromide - - - 9 grains
> Make up with cold distilled water to 20 ozs.

We make up sufficient fixing solution to fill a 'Winchester', that is an 80-oz. bottle. The formula is:

> Hypo (crystals) - - - - 20 ozs.
> Kodak Liquid Hardener - - 4 ozs.
> Water to make - - - - 80 ozs.

This solution may be used repeatedly, but should be filtered through a pad of cotton wool placed in the funnel when it is being returned to the stock bottle after use.

Suppose now we assume a case where there are few darkroom facilities, and deal with the development of a film pack under those

[1] This amount applies in the case of a 35 mm. film of 36 exposures or a 3¼″ × 2¼″ film of 8 exposures. Other sizes need replenisher in proportion to their total area.

conditions. The corresponding procedure in more favourable circumstances will be self-evident, and anyone will be able to adapt his method of working to the peculiarities of his own surroundings. The first task is to load the film into the tank, and as this must be done in total darkness, we usually do it at night. If necessary, the room is darkened by drawing the curtains or pinning a blanket across the window, and where there is still some doubt about the complete exclusion of light, we try to get into a dark corner or cupboard.

We generally dilute the concentrated 1D.2. developer with nine times its volume of water, and find this more suitable for most natural history subjects than the dilution of one part in five which is recommended by the manufacturers for general use. The 'Dallan' tanks, which we use for film packs, require 50 ozs. and 35 ozs. of solution for the $\frac{1}{4}$-plate and $3\frac{1}{2}$ by $2\frac{1}{2}$ sizes respectively, and the appropriate quantity of working solution is prepared in the jug and brought to a temperature of 68° F. In the varied conditions under which the bird photographer has to work, it may often happen that the temperature of the room will be much below the desired temperature of development, and in such cases it is important to warm the tank itself to approximately the right temperature before pouring in the developer. This is usually best achieved by standing the jug of developer and the tank in a larger vessel of warm water. We develop Selo Hypersensitive Pan. or Kodak Super XX film for 18 minutes in this developer, turning the tank upside down every three or four minutes to ensure even development. At the end of the development period the developer is run quickly out of the tank into a sink or bucket for throwing away, and, without previous rinsing of the films, the hypo, which should have been previously warmed to exactly the same temperature as the developer, is poured into the tank.

In the case of miniature negatives, the procedure is similar to the above, but we use the DK.20 developer in a Johnson's tank, developing for 12 mins. at 68° F. With these tiny films it is even more important to keep all solutions, and the final washing water, at a constant temperature. In summer, running water, where it is available, may often attain a temperature very close to 68° F., and in such cases we use it to wash the films, but where the supply is at some other temperature, we bring a bucket of water to 68° F., and, drawing from this, soak the negatives for 5 minutes in each of twelve changes of water. This method must in any case be used in many country places where water is not available on tap.

During a spell of bird photography our time is usually fully occupied, especially if flashlight work at night is added to observations and photography by day. Accordingly, the development of negatives is arranged in such a way that it interferes as little as possible with our outdoor programme or with our essential rest. We find that, so long as negatives are loaded into the tanks last thing at night and that developing and fixing solutions are made up in advance, as already suggested, the development process can be conveniently carried out while we are dressing next morning; fixing takes place while we are having breakfast; and the washing can be done during the preparation for the day's expedition. Of course, this scheme will not suit all occasions, but the general principle holds good. Even by this method it is often not possible to keep completely up to date, but we make a point of developing some exposures from each nest, and then use slack periods, which often accompany bad weather, to catch up the arrears.

Processing negatives away from home has its dangers, the greatest of which probably arise during the period of drying, and we take especial care to put them in a place that is reasonably free from dust and where they cannot readily be spoiled. For example, the good intentions of the lady of the house in opening the window in our absence, may cause damp films to blow together and stick, and may blow a cloud of dust into an otherwise suitable room, so we certainly keep our negatives well away from a window, and, if possible, put them to dry in a cupboard. After scrutiny, to discover any possible features in our work that may need improvement or correction, the negatives are carefully packed away to await printing.

Little need be said with regard to printing bird or other Nature negatives. We follow normal methods, and endeavour to get a straight print free from local shading, re-touching, or other 'control'. We find a cream base paper is usually the most pleasing, though, of course glossy black and white is better for prints that are to be reproduced. After tests with a wide range of papers of different types we have no hesitation in preferring Ilford Plastika for glossy prints, and, to obtain the rich blue-black shadows that reproduce well, we develop this in the following amidol solution

Water, to make - - - -	20 ozs.
Sodium sulphite - - - -	1 oz.
Potassium bromide - - -	6 grains
Amidol - - - - - -	50 grains

For exhibition prints we use Kodak Fine Grain Royal or Plastika semi-matt, developing the former in the amidol solution mentioned above, and the latter in the maker's formula I.D. 49, which gives warm black tones. This is made up as follows:

Metol - - - - - -	6 grains
Hydroquinone - - - -	54 grains
[1] Chlorquinol - - - - -	54 grains
Sodium sulphite (crystals) - -	4 ozs.
Sodium carbonate (crystals) - -	1¼ ozs.
Potassium bromide - - -	15 grains
Water, to make - - - -	80 ozs.

In addition to the print on paper we use the lantern slide as a means of displaying our Nature photographs. The slide has particular advantages for coping with this type of subject for it is able to render a very wide range of tones and reveals more adequately than a print the full beauty that is in the negative. A variety of colours can be produced by using different makes of lantern plate and different developers, and we recommend the adoption of a varied procedure for the sake of the interest it affords. Experiment and experience in this matter is the only sure guide to success, but as a lead to beginners we have often used Ilford Warm Tone Lantern plates in conjunction with the I.D. 49 developer already mentioned, getting our best tones with a development time of 2½ minutes at 70° F.

[1] Chlorquinol is a proprietory chemical made by Johnson & Sons Ltd., and is not generally obtainable during the war. The same weight of Glycin may be substituted, though this gives a slightly warmer tone.

And so our quest for bird photographs comes to fruition. We have had the thrill of finding the nest; the excitement of working at close quarters to our quarry; and the satisfaction of seeing it captured on to the negative. The completion of the print or slide represents the culmination of our efforts and often brings the greatest thrill of all. It gives us, moreover, a ready means to share our Nature experiences with others; to reveal to them something of the fascination of the wild that we ourselves have enjoyed. And we emphasize that word 'enjoyed', for, even though bird photography, taken seriously, is hard work and is exacting in its requirements, we find it enjoyable from first to last; and so we venture to think will any others, who, tempted by what we have written, turn their minds and hands to the 'Art of Bird Photography'.

Acknowledgments

Before bringing this book to a close, we should like to pay tribute to the many firms in the photographic and allied industries, who, by their research and development, have made possible bird photography as we know it today. Without the benefits of large aperture and telephoto lenses; of fast and colour sensitive emulsions, combined with fineness of grain; of modern flashlight; and of the innumerable high grade accessories that are available, much of our work would have been difficult, if not impossible.

Besides this, we recall with gratitude the advice and assistance we have received, in particular from Messrs. J. H. Dallmeyer Ltd., Messrs. Ilford Ltd., and Messrs. Kodak Ltd., in the matter of the selection of equipment and in any technical difficulties that have been encountered. We have, in the course of the book, referred specifically to certain items that have proved of especial value, and which we can, with confidence, recommend to other bird photographers; but it should perhaps be made quite clear that we have no connection or financial interest whatever in the concerns mentioned.

Acknowledgments   93

From certain journals and periodicals we have received a good deal of encouragement in our work, and would mention especially *Country Life*, and *The Field*, who from time to time have published accounts of our observations; and *Picture Post* which has made features of some of our Nature photographs. Apart from these, many of the great newspapers and periodicals of the country have reflected the public interest in Nature subjects, and, both directly and indirectly, have helped in furthering the study and photography of bird life.

Finally, we would mention the helpful criticism that has been accorded us by the members of the Zoological Photographic Club and the Nature Photographic Society. These bodies, by means of circulating portfolios, do much to raise the standard of Nature photography, and most of the eminent nature photographers have appeared on their membership rolls. Membership is restricted, but it should be the aim of all who aspire to the portrayal of Nature by means of the camera. The local photographic societies up and down the country, and the Royal Photographic Society with its world-wide membership, are all doing good work in the same cause; and the British Ornithologists' Union, and the British Trust for Ornithology, are fostering the science which is, after all, the background against which our bird photographs have their place.

Index

94